Python Data Science

Hands on Learning for Beginners

By

Travis Booth

Table of Contents

Introduction

Congratulations on making this purchase of *Python Data Science: Hands On Learning for Beginners!* This book will guide you through the field of Data Science from the very beginning. The purpose of it is to teach you the process of data science, while also providing you with all the fundamental skills and tools in order to support your learning process. This book is intended for complete beginners looking for a way to easily understand the basics of data science.

Learning data science with Python can be intimidating at times due to the requirements of programming and mathematical knowledge. Because of this "fear," *Python Data Science: Hands On Learning for Beginners* aims to demystify complex technical concepts. One of the main goals of this book is to explain everything at a basic level so that everyone can understand what data science is all about.

This book carefully guides you through the following topics:

In the first section you will learn how to get started. You will be guided on how to install Python together with all the packages and tools you need to assist you along the way. You will also go through a chapter about programming concepts, where you will learn about basic data types in programming and Python's syntax. There will be examples of code guiding you through each concept, with clear explanations. Because this book is aimed towards beginners curious about data science, you do not have to be a master at programming.

Next, you will learn about the structure of a basic data science project and each phase you need to go through to reach your goals. You will also learn about tools specifically used by data scientists. You will be guided on how to install them, how to prepare them for work, and how to implement them in your own projects.

In the next section, you will go through what is considered the core of data science. You will learn about the data science pipeline, how to process your data, and finally the concept of machine learning. The chapters belonging to this section include clear explanations of the theory behind every concept, and they also include live examples with real data sets.

Finally, you will also be acquainted with the concept of graphical visualization. Results can often be difficult to communicate, because on their own they can be long string of numbers that aren't easily understood by beginners. You will learn some basic tools that can help you create interactive charts and make it possible for you to share your results with others.

Keep in mind that in order to benefit the most from this book, you should work through the examples presented in each section. If you have a difficult time understanding some of them, break them apart line by line, and slowly push through them until you understand the concepts. Each chapter will teach you about the tools you need, show you how to install them, and give you enough information so that you are able to work on your own as well. Make sure to practice everything you read, because without practical work you won't succeed at fully understanding the theory.

A Note about Code and Datasets

Throughout the book we will work with algorithms, Python code, and various datasets. Math will be kept at a bare minimum, though it is necessary when we're discussing various algorithms and code blocks. All of the tools, datasets, as well as code are available for free. This book uses only open source tools and data sets that anyone can download and use freely from various sources.

This book relies on community driven tools and datasets for two important reasons. Firstly, they are free and this makes it easy for any student to have access to them. Secondly, they are extremely popular and well documented. What does that mean?

For example, we are going to have practical discussions based on datasets such as Iris, Boston housing, and others. These datasets are either part of various libraries, part of tools such as Scikit-learn, or they are available for download in public repositories. Working with these datasets allows you to compare your results with other data scientists who used them for training or study. If this book fails to help you understand something regarding one of the tools or datasets, you can do your own research on the topic and find different thoughts and opinions that might help you out.

Working with open source data also allows you to team up with other aspiring data scientists such as yourself. There are many online communities out there, and using common tools and datasets will allow you to join forces. Two heads are better than one, after all, and with the help of a partner you might have an easier time learning the more complex concepts behind data science or machine learning.

In the chapters containing these datasets and Python packages, you will be fully guided on how to install them or import them to your project. Keep in mind that you should also practice outside of the examples that are present in the book. Once you gain enough knowledge and some confidence in your ability, you will be able to start putting everything in application. Whatever you do, don't wait until you feel ready. Start as soon as possible, because starting early with exercises will significantly boost your learning process.

With that being said, let's get started and learn about Python and data science!

Chapter 1: Getting Started

Data Science might be a relatively new multi-disciplinary field, however its integral parts have been individually studied by mathematicians and IT professionals for decades. Some of these core elements include machine learning, graph analysis, linear algebra, computational linguistics, and much more. Because of this seemingly wild combination of mathematics, data communication, and software engineering, the domain of data science is highly versatile. Keep in mind that not all data scientists are the same. Each one of them specializes based on competency and area of expertise. With that in mind, you might be asking yourself now what's the most important, or powerful, tool for anyone aiming to become a data scientist.

This book will focus on the use of Python, because this tool is highly appreciated within the community of data scientists and it's easy to start with. This is a highly versatile programming language that is used in a wide variety of technical fields including software development and production. It is powerful, easy to understand, and can handle any kind of program whether small or complex.

Python started out in 1991, and it has nothing to do with snakes. As a fun fact, this programming language loved by both beginners and professionals was named this way because its creator was a big fan of Monty Python, a British comedy group. If you're also one of their fans, you might notice several references to them inside the code, as well as the language's documentation. But enough about trivia - we're going to focus on Python due to its ability to develop quick experimentations and deploy scientific application. Here are some of the other core features that explain why Python is the way to go when learning data science:

1. **Integration**: Python can integrate many other tools and even code written in other programming languages. It can act as a unifying force that brings together algorithms, data strategies, and languages.

2. **Versatility**: Are you a complete beginner who never learned any kind of programming language, whether procedural or object-oriented? No problem, Python is considered by many to be the best tool for aspiring data scientists to grasp the concepts of programming. You can start coding as soon as you learn the basics!

3. **Power**: Python offers every tool you need for data analysis and more. There are an increasing number of packages and external tools that can be imported into Python to extend its usability. The possibilities are truly endless, and that is one of the reasons why this programming language is so popular in diverse technical fields, including data science.

4. **Cross-Platform Compatibility**: Portability is not a problem no matter the platform. Programs and tools written in Python will work on Windows, Mac, as well as Linux and its many distributions.

Python is a Jack of all trades, master of everything. It easy to learn, powerful, and easy to integrate with any other tools and languages, and that is why this book will focus on it when discussing data science and its many aspects. Now let's begin by installing Python.

Installing Python

Since many aspiring data scientists never used Python before, we're going to discuss the installation process to familiarize you with various packages and distributions that you will need later.

Before we begin, it's worth taking note that there are two versions of Python, namely Python 2 and Python 3. You can use either of them, however Python 3 is the future. Many data scientists still use Python 2, but the shift to version 3 has been building up gradually. What's important to keep in mind is that there are various compatibility issues between the two versions. This means that if you write a program using Python 2 and then run it inside a Python 3 interpreter, the code might not work. The developers behind Python have also stopped focusing on Python 2, therefore version 3 is the one that is being constantly developed and improved. With that being said, let's go through the step by step installation process.

Step by Step Setup

Start by going to Python's webpage at www.python.org and download Python. Next, we will go through the manual installation which requires several steps and instructions. It is not obligatory to setup Python manually, however, this gives you great control over the installation and it's important for future installations that you will perform independently depending on each of your projects' specifications. The easier way of installing Python is through automatically installing a scientific data distribution, which sets you up with all the packages and tools you may need (including a lot that you won't need). Therefore, if you wish to go through the simplified installation method, head down to the section about scientific distributions.

When you download Python from the developer's website, make sure to choose the correct installer depending on your machine's operating system. Afterwards, simply run the installer. Python is now installed, however, it is not quite ready for our purposes. We will now have to install various packages. The easiest way to do this is to open the command console and type "pip" to bring up the package manager. The "easy_install" package manager is an alternative, but pip is widely considered an improvement. If you run the commands and nothing happens, it means that you need to download and install any of these managers. Just head to their respective websites and go through a basic installation process to get them. But why bother with a package manager as a beginner?

A package manager like "pip" will make it a lot easier for you to install / uninstall packages, or roll them back if the package version causes some incompatibility issues or errors. Because of this advantage of streamlining the process, most new Python installations come with pip pre-installed. Now let's learn how to install a package. If you chose "pip", simply type the following line in the command console:

pip install < package_name >

If you chose "Easy Install", the process remains the same. Just type:

easy_install < package_name >

Once the command is given, the specified package will be downloaded and installed together with any other dependencies they require in order to run. We will go over the most important packages that you will require in a later section. For now, it's enough to understand the basic setup process.

Scientific Distributions

As you can see in the previous section, building your working environment can be somewhat time consuming. After installing Python, you need to choose the packages you need for your project and install them one at a time. Installing many different packages and tools can lead to failed installations and errors. This can often result in a massive loss of time for an aspiring data scientist who doesn't fully understand the subtleties behind certain errors. Finding solutions to them isn't always straightforward. This is why you have the option of directly downloading and installing a scientific distribution.

Automatically building and setting up your environment can save you from spending time and frustration on installations and allow you to jump straight in. A scientific distribution usually contains all the libraries you need, an Integrated Development Environment (IDE), and various tools. Let's discuss the most popular distributions and their application.

Anaconda

This is probably the most complete scientific distribution offered by Continuum Analytics. It comes with close to 200 packages pre-installed, including Matplotlib, Scikit-learn, NumPy, pandas, and more (we'll discuss these packages a bit later). Anaconda can be used on any machine, no matter the operating system, and can be installed next to any other distributions. The purpose is to offer the user everything they need for analytics, scientific computing, and mass-processing. It's also worth mentioning that it comes with its own package manager pre-installed, ready for you to use in order to manage packages. This is a powerful distribution, and luckily it can be downloaded and installed for free, however there is an advanced version that requires purchase.

If you use Anaconda, you will be able to access "conda" in order to install, update, or remove various packages. This package manager can also be used to install virtual environments (more on that later). For now, let's focus on the commands. First, you need to make sure you are running the latest version of conda. You can check and update by typing the following command in the command line:

conda update conda

Now, let's say you know which package you want to install. Type the following command:

conda install < package_name >

If you want to install multiple packages, you can list them one after another in the same command line. Here's an example:

conda install < package_number_1 > < package_number_2 > < package_number_3 >

Next, you might need to update some existing packages. This can be done with the following command:

conda update < package_name >

You also have the ability to update all the packages at once. Simply type:

conda update --all

The last basic command you should be aware of for now is the one for package removal. Type the following command to uninstall a certain package:

conda remove < package_name >

This tool is similar to "pip" and "easy install", and even though it's usually included with Anaconda, it can also be installed separately because it works with other scientific distributions as well.

Canopy

This is another scientific distribution popular because it's aimed towards data scientists and analysts. It also comes with around 200 pre-installed packages and includes the most popular ones you will use later, such as Matplotlib and pandas. If you choose to use this distribution instead of Anaconda, type the following command to install it:

canopy_cli

Keep in mind that you will only have access to the basic version of Canopy without paying. If you will ever require its advanced features, you will have to download and install the full version.

WinPython

If you are running on a Windows operating system, you might want to give WinPython a try. This distribution offers similar features as the ones we discussed earlier, however it is community driven. This means that it's an open source tool that is entirely free.

You can also install multiple versions of it on the same machine, and it comes with an IDE pre-installed.

Virtual Environments

Virtual environments are often necessary because you are usually locked to the version of Python you installed. It doesn't matter whether you installed everything manually or you chose to use a distribution - you can't have as many installations on the same machine as you might want. The only exception would be if you are using the WinPython distribution, which is available only for Windows machines, because it allow you to prepare as many installations as you want. However, you can create a virtual environment with the "virtualenv". Create as many different installations as you need without worrying about any kind of limitations. Here are a few solid reasons why you should choose a virtual environment:

1. **Testing grounds**: It allows you to create a special environment where you can experiment with different libraries, modules, Python versions and so on. This way, you can test anything you can think of without causing any irreversible damage.

2. **Different versions**: There are cases when you need multiple installations of Python on your computer. There are packages and tools, for instance, that only work with a certain version. For instance, if you are running Windows, there are a few useful packages that will only behave correctly if you are running Python 3.4, which isn't the most recent update. Through a virtual

environment, you can run different version of Python for separate goals.

3. **Replicability**: Use a virtual environment to make sure you can run your project on any other computer or version of Python aside from the one you were originally using. You might be required to run your prototype on a certain operating system or Python installation, instead of the one you are using on your own computer. With the help of a virtual environment, you can easily replicate your project and see if it runs under different circumstances.

With that being said, let's start installing a virtual environment by typing the following command:

pip install virtualenv

This will install "virtualenv", however you will first need to make several preparations before creating the virtual environment. Here are some of the decisions you have to make at the end of the installation process:

1. **Python version**: Decide which version you want "virtualenv" to use. By default, it will pick up the one it was installed from. Therefore, if you want to use another Python version, you have to specify by typing -*p python 3.4*, for instance.

2. **Package installation**: The virtual environment tool is set to always perform the full package installation process for each environment even when you already have said package installed on your system. This can lead to a loss of time and resources. To avoid this issue, you can use the *--system-site-packages* command to instruct the tool to install the packages from the files

already available on your system.

3. **Relocation**: For some projects, you might need to move your virtual environment on a different Python setup or even on another computer. In that case, you will have to instruct the tool to make the environment scripts work on any path. This can be achieved with the *--relocatable* command.

Once you make all the above decisions, you can finally create a new environment. Type the following command:

virtualenv myenv

This instruction will create a new directory called "myenv" inside the location, or directory, where you currently are. Once the virtual environment is created, you need to launch it by typing these lines:

cd myenv

activate

Now you can start installing various packages by using any package manager like we discussed earlier in the chapter.

Necessary Packages

We discussed earlier that the advantages of using Python for data science are its system compatibility and highly developed system of packages. An aspiring data scientist will require a diverse set of tools for their projects. The analytical packages we are going to talk about have been highly polished and thoroughly tested over the years, and therefore are used by the majority of data scientists, analysts, and engineers.

Here are the most important packages you will need to install for most of your work:

1. **NumPy**: This analytical library provides the user with support for multi-dimensional arrays, including the mathematical algorithms needed to operate on them. Arrays are used for storing data, as well as for fast matrix operations that are much needed to work out many data science problems. Python wasn't meant for numerical computing, therefore every data scientist needs a package like NumPy to extend the programming language to include the use of many high level mathematical functions. Install this tool by typing the following command: *pip install numpy*.

2. **SciPy**: You can't read about NumPy without hearing about SciPy. Why? Because the two complement each other. SciPy is needed to enable the use of algorithms for image processing, linear algebra, matrices and more. Install this tool by typing the following command: *pip install scipy*.

3. **pandas**: This library is needed mostly for handling diverse data tables. Install pandas to be able to load data from any source and manipulate as needed. Install this tool by typing the following command: *pip install pandas*.

4. **Scikit**-learn: A much needed tool for data science and machine learning, Scikit is probably the most important package in your toolkit. It is required for data preprocessing, error metrics, supervised and unsupervised learning, and much more. Install this tool by typing the following command: *pip install scikit-*

learn.

5. **Matplotlib**: This package contains everything you need to build plots from an array. You also have the ability to visualize them interactively. You don't happen to know what a plot is? It is a graph used in statistics and data analysis to display the relation between variables. This makes Matplotlib an indispensable library for Python. Install this tool by typing the following command: *pip install matplotlib.*

6. **Jupyter**: No data scientist is complete without Jupyter. This package is essentially an IDE (though much more) used in data science and machine learning everywhere. Unlike IDEs such as Atom, or R Studio, Jupyter can be used with any programming language. It is both powerful and versatile because it provides the user with the ability to perform data visualization in the same environment, and allows customizable commands. Not only that, it also promotes collaboration due to its streamlined method of sharing documents. Install this tool by typing the following command: *pip install jupyter.*

7. **Beautiful Soup**: Extract information from HTML and XML files that you have access to online. Install this tool by typing the following command: *pip install beautifulsoup4.*

For now, these 7 packages should be enough to get you started and give you an idea on how to extend Python's abilities. You don't have to overwhelm yourself just yet by installing all of them, however feel free to explore and experiment on your own. We will mention and discuss more packages later in the book as needed to solve our data science problems. But for now, we need to focus more on Jupyter, because it will be used throughout the book. So let's go through the installation, special commands, and learn how this tool can help you as an aspiring data scientist.

Using Jupyter

Throughout this book, we will use Jupyter to illustrate various operations we perform and their results. If you didn't install it yet, let's start by typing the following command:

pip install jupyter

The installation itself is straightforward. Simply follow the steps and instruction you receive during the setup process. Just make sure to download the correct installer first. Once the setup finishes, we can run the program by typing the next line:

jupyter notebook

This will open an instance of Jupyter inside your browser. Next, click on "New" and select the version of Python you are running. As mentioned earlier, we are going to focus on Python 3. Now you will see an empty window where you can type your commands.

You might notice that Jupyter uses code cell blocks instead of looking like a regular text editor. That's because the program will execute code cell by cell. This allows you to test and experiment with parts of your code instead of your entire program. With that being said, let's give it a test run and type the following line inside the cell:

In: print ("I'm running a test!")

Now you can click on the play button that is located under the Cell tab. This will run your code and give you an output, and then a new input cell will appear. You can also create more cells by hitting the plus button in the menu. To make it clearer, a typical block looks something like this:

In: < This is where you type your code >

Out: < This is the output you will receive >

The idea is to type your code inside the "In" section and then run it. You can optionally type in the result you expect to receive inside the "Out" section, and when you run the code, you will see another "Out" section that displays the true result. This way you can also test to see if the code gives you the result you expect.

Chapter 2: Python Crash Course

Before we dig deeper into data science and working with Python and Jupyter, you should understand the basics of programming. If you already grasp the concepts or you have some experience with programming in Python or any other language, feel free to skip this chapter. However, even if you already possess the basic knowledge, you might want to refresh your memory.

In this chapter we're going to discuss basics programming concepts and go through simple examples that illustrate them. It is recommended that you put into practice what you read as soon as possible, even if at first you use cheat sheets. The goal here is to practice, because theory is not enough to solidify what you learn.

For the purpose of this chapter, we will not use Jupyter or any other IDE that is normally used when programming. All we need is a shell where we put our code to the test and exercise. To do that, just head to Python's main website here *https://www.python.org/shell/* and you'll be able to try everything out without installing anything on your computer.

Programming Naming Conventions

Before we start discussing programming concepts such as strings, functions, conditional statements and loops, you need to learn how to write clean, easy to understand code. Readability and consistency are vital when working on a project, especially if others have to read your work. For this reason, you need to learn about programming naming conventions. A programmer or a data analyst should be able to look through your code and understand it at a glance. It should be self-explanatory with intuitive variables that make it clear to the reader what their purpose is.

Do not ignore this aspect of programming. Someday you might write a program, hit a stump, abandon it for a short while and when you come back to it, it will look like gibberish due to variables that have no meaning to you.

With that being said, here are the most commonly used naming conventions used by programmers and data scientists:

1. **Pascal Case**: Capitalize the first letter of each word without using any spaces or symbols between them. A variable name written using Pascal Case should look something like this: PascalCaseVariable, MyComplexPassword, CarManufacturer.

2. **Camel Case**: This is almost the same as Pascal case, except the first word starts with a lowercase letter. A variable name written using Camel Case should look something like this: camelCaseVariable, myInterface, userPassword.

3. **Snake Case**: This naming convention is often used to clearly illustrate multi-word variables by separating each word with an underscore sign. Snake Case can be applied together with Camel Case or Pascal Case. The only thing that differentiates it from others is word separation. A variable name written using Snake Case should look something like this: my_snake_case_variable, This_is also_snake_case, my_account_password. Reading variable names might

seem easier on the eye by using this naming convention. As a side note, Snake Case is also great for naming your project folders and files and it is often used for that purpose.

Keep in mind that there is no such thing as the "best" naming convention. It all depends on your preference, however you should always be consistent when writing your code. Try not to mix different naming conventions. Pick one style and stick to it throughout your project. Give your variables a descriptive name that allows the reader to understand what it does and then write them by using one of the mentioned conventions.

Data Types

Understanding basic data types is essential to the aspiring data scientist. Python has several in-built data types, and in this section we will discuss each one of them. Remember to follow along with the exercises and try to use the bits of knowledge you gain to come up with your own lines of code.

Here are the most important data types we will be discussing: numbers, strings, dictionaries, lists, and tuples. Start up your Python shell and let's begin!

Numbers

In programming and mathematics, there are several types of numbers, and you need to specify them in Python when writing code. You have integers, floats, longs, complex numbers, and a few more. The ones you will use most often, however, are integers and floats.

An integer (written as "int" in Python) is a positive or negative whole number. That means that when you declare an integer, you cannot use a number with decimal points. If you need to use decimals, however, you declare a float.

In Python, there are several mathematical operators that you can use to make various calculations using integers and floats. The arithmetic operators are for adding (+), subtracting (-), multiplication (*), division (/), modulus (%), floor division (//) and exponent (**). There are also comparison operators such as greater than (>), less than (<), equal to (==), not equal to (!=), greater than or equal to (>=) and less than or equal to (<=). These are the basic operators, and they are included with any Python installation. There's no need to install a package or a module for them. Now let's try a simple exercise to put some of these operators in action.

x = 100

y = 25

print (x + y)

This simple operation will print the result of x + y. You can use any of the other arithmetic operators this way. Play around with them and create complex equations if you want to. The process is the same. Now let's look at an example of comparison operators:

x = 100

y = 25

print (x > 100)

The result you will see is "false" because our declared x

variable is not greater than y. Now let's move on to strings!

Strings

Strings are everything that is in text format. You can declare anything as simple textual information, such as letters, numbers, or punctuation signs. Keep in mind that numbers written as strings are not the same as numbers used as variables. To write a string, simply type whatever you want to type in-between quotation marks. Here's an example

x = "10"

In this case, x is a string and not an integer.

So what are strings for? They are used frequently in programming, so let's see some of the basic operations in action. You can write code to determine the character length of a line of text, to concatenate, or for iteration. Here's an example:

len("hello")

The result you get is 5, because the "len" function is used to return the length of this string. The word "hello" is made of 5 characters, therefore the calculation returns 5 to the console. Now let's see how concatenation looks. Type the following instruction:

'my' + 'stubborn' + 'cat'

The result will be mystubborncat, without any spaces in between the words. Why? Because we didn't add any spaces inside the strings. A space is considered as a character. Try writing it like this:

'my ' + 'stubborn ' + 'cat'

Now the result will be "my stubborn cat". By the way, did you realize we changed the quotation marks to single quotes? The code still performed as intended, because Python can't tell the difference between the two. You can use both double quotes and single quotes as you prefer, and it will have no impact on your code.

Now let's see an example of string iteration. Type:

movieTitle = "Star Wars"

for c in movie: print c,

...

These lines of code will return all individual characters in the declared string. We first declare a variable called "movieTitle" to which we assign "Star Wars" as its string. Next we call to print each character within the "movieTitle.

There are other string operations that you can perform with Python, however for the purposes of this book it's enough to stick to the basics. If you wish, you can always refer to Python's online documentation and read all the information they have on strings. Next up, let's discuss lists!

Lists

Lists are incredibly useful in programming, and you will have to use them often in your work. If you are familiar with object oriented programming languages, Python lists are in fact identical to arrays. You can use them to store data, manipulate it on demand, and store different objects in them and so on.

Using them in Python is simple, so let's first see how to make a new list. Type the following line:

x = [1, 2, 3, 4, 5, 6, 7, 8, 9, 10]

The list is created by declaring a series of objects enclosed by square brackets. As we already mentioned, list don't have to contain only one data type. You can store any kind of information in them. Here's another example of a list:

myBook = ["title", "somePages", 1, 2, 3, 22, 42, "bookCover"]

As you can see, we are creating a list that contains both strings and numbers. Next up, you can start performing all the operations you used for strings. They work the same with lists. For instance, here's how you can concatenate the two previous lists we created:

x + myBook

Here's the result:

[1, 2, 3, 4, 5, 6, 7, 8, 9, 10, "title", "somePages", 1, 2, 3, 22, 42, "bookCover"]

Try out any other operation yourself and see what happens. Explore and experiment with what you already know.

Dictionaries

Dictionaries are similar to lists, however you need to have a key that is associated with the objects inside. You use the key to access those objects. Let's explain this through an example in order to avoid any confusion. Type the following lines:

dict = {'weapon' : 'sword', 'soldier' : 'archer'}

dict ['weapon']

As you can see, in the first line we declared a dictionary. It is defined between two curly brackets, and inside it contains objects with a key assigned to each of them. For instance, we have object "sword" that has the "weapon" as its attributed key. In order to access the "sword" we have to call on its key, which we do in the second line of code. Keep in mind that the "weapon" or "soldier" keys are only examples. Keys don't have to be strings. You can use anything.

Tuples

Tuples are also similar to lists, however their objects can't be changed after they are set. Let's see an example of a tuple and then discuss it. Type the following line:

x = (1, 2, 'someText', 99, [1, 2, 3])

The tuple is in between parentheses and it contains three data types. There are three integers, a string, and a list. You can now perform any operation you want on the tuple. Try the same commands you used for lists and strings. They will work with tuples as well because they are so similar. The only real difference is that once you declare the elements inside a tuple, you cannot modify them through code. If you have some knowledge about object oriented programming, you might notice that Python tuples are similar to constants.

Python Code Structure

Now that you know some basic data types, we can discuss Python's code structure before progressing with statements, loops, and more. Python uses whitespace or indentation in order to organize code blocks into readable and executable programs. If you do not respect the indentation, you will receive an indentation error. Other languages such as those that are heavily based on the C use curly brackets to mark the beginning and end of a code block. Let's see this difference through an example. This is what a C code block would look like:

```
if ( x == 100)

{

        printf ("x is 100");

        printf ("moving on");

}

printf ("there's nothing else to declare");
```

As you can see, we have curly braces to mark the borders of a code block. There's also another key difference. In Python, there's no need to use semicolons to mark the end of a line of code. Here's the same block of code, but written in Python:

```
if x == 100 :

        print ("x is 100")

        print ("moving on")

print ("there's nothing else to declare")
```

Notice how in Python the contents of the "if" statement are indented. That's what tells the program that those lines belong to the statement above. If you type in Python something like this:

```
if x == 100 :

print ("x is 100")

print ("moving on")

print ("there's nothing else to declare")
```

The result will look like this:

```
IndentationError: unexpected indent
```

So whenever you write code in Python, make sure you make the appropriate use of whitespace to define the code blocks. Simply press the "tab" key on your keyboard to indent as needed.

Another thing worth mentioning here is the use of parentheses in the "if" statement that we declared in our example. In the C version of the code we used them, however in the Python version we ignored them. While in Python you don't have to use those parentheses, you should. They are optional, but they make the code easier to read and understand. It is widely accepted in the programming world that using them is best practice, so you should learn how to write clean code from the beginning.

Conditional Statements

This is the part when things start to get fun. Conditional statements are used to give your program some ability to think and decide on their own what they do with the data they receive. They are used to analyze the condition of a variable and instruct the program to react based on values. We already used the most common conditional statement in the example above.

Statements in Python programming are as logical as those you make in the real world when making decisions. "If I'm sick tomorrow, I will skip school, else I will just have to go" is a simple way of describing how the "if" statement above works. You tell the program to check whether you are sick tomorrow. If it returns a false value, because you aren't sick, then it will continue to the "else" statement which tells you to go to school because you aren't sick. "If" and "if, else" conditional statements are a major part of programming. Now let's see how they look in code:

```
x = 100

if (x < 100):

        print("x is small")
```

This is the basic "If" statement with no other conditions. It simply examines if the statement is true. You declared the value of x to be 100. If x is smaller than 100, the program will print "x is small". In our case, the statement is false and nothing will happen because we didn't tell the program what to do in such a scenario. Let's extend this code by typing:

```
x = 100

if (x < 100):

        print("x is small")

else:

        print("x is big")

print ("This part will be returned whatever the result")
```

Now that we introduced the "else" statement, we are telling the program what to execute if the statement that "x is smaller than 100" is not true. At the end of the code block, we also added a separate line outside of the "if else" statement and it will return the result without considering any of the conditions. Pay special attention to the indentation here. The last line is not considered as part of the "if" and "else" statements because of the way we wrote it.

But what if you want your program to check for several statements and do something based on the results? That's when the "elif" conditional comes in. Here's how the syntax would look:

if (condition1):

      add a statement here

elif (condition2):

      add another statement for this condition

elif (condition3):

      add another statement for this condition

else:

      if none of the conditions apply, do this

As you may have noticed, we haven't exactly used code to express how the "elif" statement is used. What we did instead was write what is known as pseudo code. Pseudo code is useful when you quickly want to write the logic of your code without worrying about using code language. This makes it easier to focus on how your code is supposed to work and see if your thinking is correct. Once you write your pseudo code and decide it's the correct path to take, you can replace it with actual code. Here's how to use elif with real code:

```
x = 10

if (x > 10):

        print ("x is larger than ten")

elif x < 4:

        print ("x is a smaller number")

else:

        print ("x is not that big")
```

Now that you know how conditionals work, start practicing. Use strings, lists and operators, followed by statements that use that data. You don't need more than basic foundations to start programming. The sooner you nudge yourself in the right direction, the easier you will learn.

Logical Operators

Sometimes you need to make comparisons when using conditional statements, and that's what logical operators are for. There are three types: and, or, and not. We use the "and" operator to receive a certain result if both of them are checked to be true. The "or" operator will return a result if only one of the specified statements are true. Finally, the "not" operator is used to reverse the result.

Let's see an example of a logical operator used in a simple "if" statement. Type the following code:

```
y = 100
```

if y < 200 and y > 1:

      print("y is smaller than 200 and bigger than 1")

The program will check if the value of y is smaller than 200, as well as bigger than 1 and if both statements are true, a result will be printed.

Introduce logical operators when you practice your conditionals. You can come up with many operations because there's no limit to how many statements you can make or how many operators you use.

Loops

Sometimes we need to tell the program to repeat a set of instructions every time it meets a condition. To achieve this, we have two kinds of loops, known as the "for" loop and the "while" loop. Here's an example of a "for" loop:

for x in range(1, 10):

print(x)

In this example, we instruct our program to keep repeating until every value of x between 1 and 10 is printed. When the printed value is 2, for instance, the program checks if x is still within the (1, 10) range and if the condition is true, it will print the next number, and the next and so on.

Here's an example with a string:

for x in "programming":

      print (x)

The code will be executed repeatedly until all characters inside the word "programming" are printed.

Here's another example using a list of objects:

medievalWeapons = ["swords", "bows", "spears", "throwing axes"]

for x in medievalWeapons:

    print(x)

In this case, the program will repeat the set of instructions until every object inside the list we declared is printed.

Next up we have the "while" loop that is used to repeat the code only as long as a condition is true. When a statement no longer meets the condition we set, the loop will break and the program will continue the next lines of code after the loop. Here's an example:

x = 1

while x < 10:

    print(x)

    x += 1

First we declare that x is an integer with the value of 1. Next we instruct the program that while x is smaller than 10 it should keep printing the result. However, we can't end the loop with just this amount of information. If we leave it at that, we will create an infinite loop because x is set to always be 1 and that means that x will forever be smaller than. The "x+= 1" at the end tells the program to increase x's value by 1 every single time the loop is executed. This means that at one point x will no longer be smaller than 10, and therefore the statement will no longer be true. The loop will finish executing, and the rest of the program will continue.

But what about that risk of running into infinite loops? Sometimes accidents happen, and we create an endless loop. Luckily, this is preventable by using a "break" statement at the end of the block of code. This is how it would look:

```
while True:

        answer = input ("Type command:")

        if answer == "Yes":

                break
```

The loop will continue to repeat until the correct command is used. In this example, you break out of the loop by typing "Yes". The program will keep running the code until you give it the correct instruction to stop.

Functions

Now that you know enough basic programming concepts, we can discuss making your programs more efficient, better optimized, and easier to analyze. Functions are used to reduce the number of lines of code that are actually doing the same thing. It is generally considered best practice to not repeat the same code more than twice. If you have to, you need to start using a function instead. Let's take a look at what a function looks like in code:

```
def myFunction():

        print("Hello, I'm your happy function!")
```

We declare a function with the "def" keyword, which contains a simple string that will be printed whenever the function is called. The defined functions are called like this:

myFunction()

You type the name of function followed by two parentheses. Now, these parentheses don't always have to stay empty. They can be used to pass parameters to the function. What's a parameter? It's simply a variable that becomes part of the function's definition. Let's take a look at an example to make things clearer:

def myName(firstname):

    print(firstname + " Johnson")

myName("Andrew")

myName("Peter")

myName("Samuel")

In this example we use the parameter "firstname" in the function's definition. We then instruct the function to always print the information inside the parameter, plus the word "Johnson". After defining the function, we call it several times with different "firstname". Keep in mind that this is an extremely crude example. You can have as many parameters as you want. By defining functions with all the parameters you need, you can significantly reduce the amount of code you write.

Now let's examine a function with a set default parameter. A default parameter will be called when you don't specify any other information in its place. Let's go through an example for a better explanation. Nothing beats practice and visualization.

Type the following code:

```
def myHobby(hobby = "leatherworking"):

        print ("My hobby is " + hobby)

myHobby ("archery")

myHobby ("gaming")

myHobby ()

myHobby ("fishing")
```

These are the results you should receive when calling the function:

My hobby is archery

My hobby is gaming

My hobby is leatherworking

My hobby is fishing

Here you can see that the function without a parameter will use the default value we set.

Finally, let's discuss a function that returns values. So far our functions were set to perform something, such as printing a string. We can't do much with these results. However, a returned value can be reassigned to a variable and used in more complex operations. Here's an example of a return function:

```
def square(x):

        return x * x

print(square (5))
```

We defined the function and then we used the "return" command to return the value of the function, which in this example is the square of 5.

Code Commenting

We discussed earlier that maintaining a clear, understandable code is one of your priorities. On top of naming conventions, there's another way you can help yourself and others understand what your code does. This is where code commenting comes in to save the day.

Few things are worse than abandoning a project for a couple of weeks and coming back to it only to stare at it in confusion. In programming, you constantly evolve, so the code you thought was brilliant a while back will seem like it's complete nonsense. Luckily, Python gives you the ability to leave text-based comments anywhere without having any kind of negative effect on the code. Comments are ignored by the program, and you can use them to briefly describe what a certain block of code is meant to achieve. A comment in Python is marked with a hashtag (#).

This is my comment.

Python disregards everything that is written after a hash symbol. You can comment before a line of code, after it, or even in the middle of it (though this is not recommended). Here's an example of this in action:

print ("This is part of the program and will be executed") #This is a comment

Comments don't interfere with the program in any way, but you should pay attention to how you express yourself and how you write the comment lines. First of all, comments should not be written in an endless line - you should break them up into several lines to make them easy to read. Secondly, you should only use them to write a short, concise description. Don't be more detailed than you have to be.

Here's how a longer comment line should look like.

Keep it simple, readable and to the point

without describing obvious data types and variables.

Get used to using comments throughout your code early one. Other programmers or data scientists will end up reading it someday, and comments make it much easier for them to understand what you wanted to accomplish. Every programmer has a different way of solving a problem, and not everyone thinks the same way, even if they arrive at the same conclusion. In the long run, good comments will save you a lot of headaches, and those who read your code may hate you a little less.

Chapter 3: Data Munging

Now that you've gone through a Python programming crash course and you have some idea of the basic concepts behind programming, we can start discussing the data science process.

So what does "data munging" even mean? A few decades ago, a group of MIT students came up with this term. Data munging is about changing some original data to more useful data by taking very specific steps. This is basically the data science pipeline. You might sometimes hear about this term being referred to as data preparation, or sometimes even data wrangling. Know that they are all synonyms.

In this chapter we're going to discuss the data science process and learn how to upload data from files, deal with missing data, as well as manipulate it.

The Process

All data science projects are different one way or another, however they can all be broken down into typical stages. The very first step in this process is acquiring data. This can be done in many ways. Your data can come from databases, HTML, images, Excel files, and many other sources, and uploading data is an important step every data scientist needs to go through.

Data munging comes after uploading the data, however at the moment that raw data cannot be used for any kind of analysis. Data can be chaotic, and filled with senseless information or gaps. This is why, as an aspiring data scientist, you solve this problem with the use of Python data structures that will turn this data into a data set that contains variables. You will need these data sets when working with any kind of statistical or machine learning analysis. Data munging might not be the most exciting phase in data science, but it is the foundation for your project and much needed to extract the valuable data you seek to obtain.

In the next phase, once you observe the data you obtain, you will begin to create a hypothesis that will require testing. You will examine variables graphically, and come up with new variables. You will use various data science methodologies such as machine learning or graph analysis in order to establish the most effective variables and their parameters. In other words, in this phase you process all the data you obtain from the previous phase and you create a model from it. You will undoubtedly realize in your testing that corrections are needed and you will return to the data munging phase to try something else. It's important to keep in mind that most of the time, the solution for your hypothesis will be nothing like the actual solution you will have at the end of a successful project. This is why you cannot work purely theoretically. A good data scientist is required to prototype a large variety of potential solutions and put them all to the test until the best course of action is revealed.

One of the most essential parts of the data science process is visualizing the results through tables, charts, and plots. In data science, this is referred to as "OSEMN", which stands for "Obtain, Scrub, Explore, Model, Interpret". While this abbreviation doesn't entirely illustrate the process behind data science, it captures the most important stages you should be aware of as an aspiring data scientist. Just keep in mind that data munging will often take the majority of your efforts when working on a project.

Importing Datasets with pandas

Now is the time to open the toolset we discussed earlier and take out pandas. We need pandas to first start by loading the tabular data, such as spreadsheets and databases, from any files. This tool is great because it will create a data structure where every row will be indexed, variables kept separate by delimiters, data can be converted, and more. Now start running Jupyter, and we'll discuss more about pandas and CSV files. Type:

In: import pandas as pd

iris_filename = 'datasets-ucl-iris.csv'

iris = pd.read_csv(iris_filename, sep=',', decimal='.', header=None,

names= ['sepal_length', 'sepal_width', 'petal_length', 'petal_width', 'target'])

We start by important pandas and naming our file. In the third line we can define which character should be used a separator with the "sep" keyword, as well as the decimal character with the "decimal" keyword. We can also specify whether there's a header with the "header" keyword, which in our case is set to none. The result of what we have so far is an object that we named "iris" and we refer to it as a pandas DataFrame. In some ways it's similar to the lists and dictionaries we talked about in Python, however there are many more features. You can explore the object's content just to see how it looks for now by typing the following line:

In: iris.head()

As you can see, we aren't using any parameters with these commands, so what you should get is a table with only the first 5 rows, because that's the default if there are no arguments. However, if you want a certain number of rows to be displayed, simply type the instruction like this:

iris.head(3)

Now you should see the first three rows instead. Next, let's access the column names by typing:

In: iris.columns

Out: Index(['sepal_length', 'sepal_width', 'petal_length',

'petal_width', 'target'], dtype='object')

The result of this will be a pandas index of the column names that looks like a list. Let's extract the target column. You can do it like this:

In: Y = iris['target']

Y

Out:

0   Iris-setosa

1   Iris -setosa

2   Iris -setosa

3   Iris -setosa

...

149   Iris-virginica

Name: target, dtype: object

For now it's important only to understand that Y is a pandas series. That means it is similar to an array, but in this case it's one directional. Another thing that we notice in this example is that the pandas Index class is just like a dictionary index. Now let's type the following:

In: X = iris[['sepal_length', 'sepal_width']]

All we did now was asking for a list of columns by index. By doing so, we received a pandas dataframe as the result. In the first example, we received a one dimensional pandas series. Now we have a matrix instead, because we requested multiple columns. What's a matrix? If your basic math is a bit rusty, you should know that it is an array of numbers that are arranged in rows and columns.

Next, we want to have the dimensions of the dataset:

In: print (X.shape)

Out: (150, 2)

In: print (Y.shape)

Out: (150,)

What we have now is a tuple. We can now see the size of the array in both dimensions. Now that you know the basics of this process, let's move on to basic preprocessing.

Preprocessing Data with pandas

The next step after learning how to load datasets is to get accustomed to the data preprocessing routines. Let's say we want to apply a function to a certain section of rows. To achieve this, we need a mask. What's a mask? It's a series of true or false values (Boolean) that we need to tell when a certain line is selected. As always, let's examine an example because reading theory can be dry and confusing.

In: mask_feature = iris['sepal_length'] > 6.0

In: mask_feature

0	False
1	False
...	
146	True
147	True
148	True
149	False

In this example we're trying to select all the lines of our "iris" dataset that have the value of "sepal length" larger than 6. You can clearly see the observations that are either true or false, and therefore know the ones that fit our query. Now let's use a mask in order to change our "iris-virginica" target with a new label. Type:

In: mask_target = iris['target'] == 'Iris-virginica'

In: iris.loc[mask_target, 'target'] = 'New label'

All "Iris-virginica" labels will now be shown as "New label" instead. We are using the "loc()" method to access this data with row and column indexes. Next, let's take a look at the new label list in the "target" column. Type:

In: iris['target'].unique()

Out: array(['Iris-setosa', 'Iris-versicolor', 'New label'], dtype=object)

In this example we are using the "unique" method to examine the new list. Next we can check the statistics by grouping every column. Let's see this in action first, and then discuss how it works. Type:

In: grouped_targets_mean = iris.groupby(['target']).mean()

grouped_targets_mean

Out:

In: grouped_targets_var = iris.groupby(['target']).var()

grouped_targets_var

Out:

We start by grouping each column with the "groupby" method. If you are a bit familiar with SQL, it's worth noting that this works similarly to the "GROUP BY" instruction. Next, we use the "mean" method, which computes the average of the values. This is an aggregate method that can be applied to one or several columns. Then we can have several other pandas methods such as "var" which stands for the variance, "sum" for the summation, "count" for the number of rows, and more. Keep in mind that the result you are looking at is still a data frame. That means that you can link as many operations as you want. In our example we are using the "groupby" method to group the observations by label and then check what the difference is between the values and variances for each of our groups.

Now let's assume the dataset contains a time series. What's a time series, you ask? In data science, sometimes we have to analyze a series of data points that are graphed in a certain chronological order. In other words, it is a sequence of the equally spaced points in time. Time series' are used often in statistics, for weather forecasting, and for counting sunspots. Often, these datasets have really noisy data points, so we have to use a "rolling" operation, like this:

In: smooth_time_series = pd.rolling_mean(time_series, 5)

As you can see, we're using the "mean" method again in order to obtain the average of values. You can also replace this method with "median" instead in order to get the median of values. In this example, we also specified that we want to obtain 5 samples.

Now let's explore pandas "apply" method that has many uses due to its ability to perform programmatically operations on rows and columns. Let's see this in action by counting the number of non-zero elements that exist in each line.

In: iris.apply(np.count_nonzero, axis=1).head()

Out: 0   5

1   5

2   5

3   5

4   5

dtype: int64

Lastly, let's use the "applymap" method for element level operations. In the next example, we are going to assume we want the length of the string representation of each cell. Type:

In: iris.applymap(lambda el:len(str(el))).head()

To receive our value, we need to cast every individual cell to a string value. Once that is done, we can gain the value of the length.

Data Selection with pandas

The final section about working with pandas is data selection. Let's say you find yourself in a situation where your dataset has an index column, and you need to import it and then manipulate it. To visualize this, let's say we have a dataset with an index from 100. Here's how it would look:

n,val1,val2,val3

100,10,10,C

101,10,20,C

102,10,30,B

103,10,40,B

104,10,50,A

So the index of row 0 is 100. If you import such a file, you will have an index column like in our case labeled as "n". There's nothing really wrong with it, however you might use the index column by mistake, so you should separate it instead in order to prevent such errors from happening. To avoid possible issues and errors, all you need to do is mention that "n" is an index column. Here's how to do it:

In: dataset = pd.read_csv('a_selection_example_1.csv',

index_col=0) dataset

Out:

Your index column should now be separate. Now let's access the value inside any cell. There's more than one way to do that. You can simply target it by mentioning the column and line. Let's assume we want to obtain "Val3" from the 5th line, which is marked by an index of 104.

In: dataset['val3'][104]

Out: 'A'

Keep in mind that this isn't a matrix, even though it might look like one. Make sure to specify the column first, and then the row in order to extract the value from the cell you want.

Categorical and Numerical Data

Now that we've gone through some basics with pandas, let's learn how to work with the most common types of data, which are numerical and categorical.

Numerical data is quite self-explanatory, as it deals with any data expressed in numbers, such as temperature or sums of money. These numbers can either be integers or floats that are defined with operators such as greater or less than.

Categorical data, on the other hand, is expressed by a value that can't be measured. A great example of this type of data, which is sometimes referred to as nominal data, is the weather, which holds values such as sunny, partially cloudy, and so on. Basically, data to which you cannot apply equal to, greater than, or less than operators is nominal data. Other examples of this data include products you purchase from an online store, computer IDs, IP addresses, etc. Booleans are the one thing that is needed to work with both categorical and numerical data. They can even be used to encode categorical values as numerical values. Let's see an example:

Categorical_feature = sunny   numerical_features = [1, 0, 0, 0, 0]

Categorical_feature = foggy   numerical _features = [0, 1, 0, 0, 0]

Categorical_feature = snowy   numerical _features = [0, 0, 1, 0, 0]

Categorical_feature = rainy   numerical _features = [0, 0, 0, 1, 0]

Categorical_feature = cloudy   numerical _features = [0, 0, 0, 0, 1]

Here we take our earlier weather example that takes the categorical data which is in the form of sunny, foggy, etc, and encode them to numerical data. This turns the information into a map with 5 true or false statements for each categorical feature we listed. One of the numerical features (1) confirms the categorical feature, while the other four are 0. Now let's turn this result into a dataframe that presents each categorical feature as a column and the numerical features next to that column. To achieve this you need to type the following code:

In: import pandas as pd

categorical_feature = pd.Series(['sunny', 'foggy', 'snowy', 'rainy', 'cloudy'])

mapping = pd.get_dummies(categorical_feature)

mapping

Out:

In data science, this is called binarization. We do not use one categorical feature with as many levels as we have. Instead, we create all the categorical features and assign two binary values to them. Next we can map the categorical values to a list of numerical values. This is how it would look:

In: mapping['sunny']

Out:

0   1.0

1   0.0

2   0.0

3   0.0

4   0.0

Name: sunny, dtype: float64

In: mapping['foggy']

Out:

0   0.0

1   1.0

2   0.0

3   0.0

4   0.0

Name: cloudy, dtype: float64

You can see in this example that the categorical value "sunny" is mapped to the following list of Booleans: 1, 0, 0, 0, 0 and you can go on like this for all the other values.

Next up, let's discuss scraping the web for data.

Scraping the Web

You won't always work with already established data sets. So far in our examples, we assumed we already had the data we needed and worked with it as it was. Often, you will have to scrape various web pages to get what you're after and download it. Here are a few real world situations where you will find the need to scrape the web:

1. In finance, many companies and institutions need to scrape the web in order to obtain up to date information about all the organizations in their portfolio. They perform this process on websites belonging to newspaper agencies, social networks, various blogs, and other corporations.

2. Did you use a product comparison website lately to find out where to get the best deal? Well, those websites need to constantly scrape the web in order to update the situation on the market's prices, products, and

services.

3. How do advertising companies figure out whether something is popular among people? How do they quantify the feelings and emotions involved with a particular product, service, or even political debate? They scrape the web and analyze the data they find in order to understand people's responses. This enables them to predict how the majority of consumers will respond under similar circumstances.

As you can see, web scraping is necessary when working with data, however working directly with web pages can be difficult because of the different people, server locations, and languages that are involved in creating websites. However, data scientists can rejoice because all websites have one thing in common, and that is HTML. For this reason, web scraping tools focus almost exclusively on working with HTML pages. The most popular tool that is used in data science for this purpose is called Beautiful Soup, and it is written in Python.

Using a tool like Beautiful Soup comes with many advantages. Firstly it enables you to quickly understand and navigate HTML pages. Secondly, it can detect errors and even fill in gaps found in the HTML code of the website. Web designers and developers are humans, after all, and they make mistakes when creating web pages. Sometimes those mistakes can turn into noisy or incomplete data, however Beautiful Soup can rectify this problem.

Keep in mind that Beautiful Soup isn't a crawler that goes through websites to index and copy all their web pages. You simply need to import and use the "urllib" library to download the code behind a webpage, and later import Beautiful Soup to read the data and run it through a parser. Let's first start by downloading a web page.

In: import urllib.request

url = 'https://en.wikipedia.org/wiki/Marco_Polo'

request = urllib.request.Request(url)

response = urllib.request.urlopen(request)

With this request, we download the code behind Wikipedia's Marco Polo web page. Next up, we use Beautiful Soup to read and parse the resources through its HTML parser.

In: from bs4 import BeautifulSoup

soup = BeautifulSoup(response, 'html.parser')

Now let's extract the web page's title like so:

In: soup.title

Out: <title>Marco Polo - Wikipedia, the free encyclopedia</title>

As you can see, we extracted the HTML title tag, which we can use further for investigation. Let's say you want to know which categories are linked to the wiki page about Marco Polo. You would need to first analyze the page to learn which HTML tag contains the information we want. There is no automatic way of doing this because web information, especially on Wikipedia, constantly changes. You have to analyze the HTML page manually to learn in which section of the page the categories are stored. How do you achieve that? Simply navigate to the Marco Polo webpage, press the F12 key to bring up the web inspector, and go through the code manually. For our example, we find the categories inside a div tag called "mw-normal-catlinks". Here's the code required to print each category and how the output would look:

In:

section = soup.find_all(id='mw-normal-catlinks')[0]

for catlink in section.find_all("a")[1:]:

print(catlink.get("title"), "->", catlink.get("href"))

Out:

Category:Marco Polo -> /wiki/Category:Marco_Polo

Category:1254 births -> /wiki/Category:1254_births

Category:1324 deaths -> /wiki/Category:1324_deaths

Category:13th-century explorers -> /wiki/Category:13thcentury_explorers

Category: 13th-century venetian people - >/wiki/Category:13thcentury_venetian_people

Category:13th-century venetian writers->/wiki/Category: 13thcentury_venetian_writers

Category:14th-century Italian writers->/wiki/Category: 14thcentury_Italian_writers

In this example, we use the "find all" method to find the HTML text contained in the argument. The method is used twice because we first need to find an ID, and secondly we need to find the "a" tags.

A word of warning when it comes to web scraping- be careful, because it is not always permitted to perform scraping. You might need authorization, because to some websites this minor invasion seems similar to a DoS attack. This confusion can lead the website to ban your IP address. So if you download data this way, read the website's terms and conditions section, or simply contact the moderators to gain more information. Whatever you do, do not try to extract information that is copyrighted. You might find yourself in legal trouble with the website / company owners.

With that being said, let's put pandas away, and look at data processing by using NumPy.

NumPy and Data Processing

Now that you know the basics of loading and preprocessing data with the help of pandas, we can move on to data processing with NumPy. The purpose of this stage is to have a data matrix ready for the next stage, which involves supervised and unsupervised machine learning mechanisms. NumPy data structure comes in the form of ndarray objects, and this is what you will later feed into the machine learning process. For now, we will start by creating such an object to better understand this phase.

The n-dimensional Array

As we discussed in the chapter about Python fundamental data types, lists and dictionaries are some of Python's most important structures. You can build complex data structures with them because they are powerful at storing data, however they're not great at operating on that data. They aren't optimal when it comes to processing power and speed, which are critical when working with complex algorithms. This is why we're using NumPy and its ndarray object, which stands for an "n-dimensional array". Let's look at the properties of a NumPy array:

1. It is optimal and fast at transferring data. When you work with complex data, you want the memory to handle it efficiently instead of being bottlenecked.

2. You can perform vectorization. In other words, you can make linear algebra computations and specific element operations without being forced to use "for" loops. This is a large plus for NumPy because Python "for" loops cost a lot of resources, making it really expensive to work with a large number of loops instead of ndarrays.

3. In data science operations you will have to use tools, or libraries, such as SciPy and Scikit-learn. You can't use them without arrays because they are required as an input, otherwise functions won't perform as intended.

With that being said, here's a few methods of creating a ndarray:

1. Take an already existing data structure and turn into an array.

2. Build the array from the start and add in the values later.

3. You can also upload data to an array even when it's stored on a disk.

Converting a list to a one-dimensional array is a fairly common operation in data science processes. Keep in mind that you have to take into account the type of objects such a list contains. This will have an impact on the dimensionality of the result. Here's an example of this with a list that contains only integers:

In: import numpy as np

int_list = [1,2,3]

Array_1 = np.array(int_list)

In: Array_1

Out: array([1, 2, 3])

You can access the array just like you access a list in Python. You simply use indexing, and just like in Python, it starts from 0. This is how this operation would look:

In: Array_1[1]

Out: 2

Now you can gain more data about the objects inside the array like so:

In: type(Array_1)

Out: numpy.ndarray

In: Array_1.dtype

Out: dtype('int64')

The result of the dtype is related to the type of operating system you're running. In this example, we're using a 64 bit operating system.

At the end of this exercise, our basic list is transformed into a uni-dimensional array. But what happens if we have a list that contains more than just one type of element? Let's say we have integers, strings, and floats. Let's see an example of this:

In: import numpy as np

composite_list = [1,2,3] + [1.,2.,3.] + ['a','b','c']

Array_2 = np.array(composite_list[:3])   #here we have only integers

print ('composite_list[:3]', Array_2.dtype)

Array_2 = np.array(composite _list[:6])   #now we have integers and floats

print (' composite _list[:6]', Array_2.dtype)

Array_2 = np.array(composite _list)   #strings have been added to the array

print (' composite _list[:] ',Array_2.dtype)

Out:

composite _list[:3] int64

composite _list[:6] float64

composite _list[:] <U32

As you can see, we have a "composite_list" that contains integers, floats, and strings. It's important to understand that when we make an array, we can have any kind of data types and mix them however we wish.

Next, let's see how we can load an array from a file. N-dimensional arrays can be created from the data contained inside a file. Here's an example in code:

In: import numpy as np

cars = np.loadtxt('regression-datasets

cars.csv',delimiter=',', dtype=float)

In this example, we tell our tool to create an array from a file with the help of the "loadtxt" method by giving it a filename, delimiter, and a data type. It's important to pay attention to the data type (dtype) because if we request a float, but the file contains a string instead, we will receive an error that tells us we cannot convert the string to a float.

Interacting with pandas

Pandas is built on NumPy and they are meant to be used together. This makes it extremely easy to extract arrays from the data frames. Once these arrays are extracted, they can be turned into data frames themselves. Let's take a look at an example:

In: import pandas as pd

import numpy as np

marketing_filename = 'regression-datasets-marketing.csv'

marketing = pd.read_csv(marketing _filename, header=None)

In this phase we are uploading data to a data frame. Next, we're going to use the "values" method in order to extract an array that is of the same type as those contained inside the data frame.

In: marketing _array = marketing.values

marketing _array.dtype

Out: dtype('float64')

We can see that we have a float type array. You can anticipate the type of the array by first using the "dtype" method. This will establish which types are being used by the specified data frame object. Do this before extracting the array. This is how this operation would look:

In: marketing.dtypes

Out: 0   float64

1   int64

2   float64

3   int64

4   float64

5   float64

6   float64

7   float64

8   int64

9   int64

10   int64

11   float64

12   float64

13   float64

dtype: object

Matrix Operations

As a data scientist, you will often have to perform multiplication on two dimensional arrays. This includes matrix calculations, such as matrix to matrix multiplication. Let's create a two dimensional array. Here's how the code and output would look:

In: import numpy as np

M = np.arange(5*5, dtype=float).reshape(5,5)

M

Out:

```
array([[     0.,    1.,    2.,    3.,    4.],
       [     5.,    6.,    7.,    8.,    9.],
       [    10.,   11.,   12.,   13.,   14.],
       [    15.,   16.,   17.,   18.,   19.],
       [    20.,   21.,   22.,   23.,   24.]])
```

This is a two dimensional array of numbers from 0 to 24. Next, we will declare a vector of coefficients and a column that will stack the vector and its reverse. Here's what it would look like:

In: coefs = np.array([1., 0.5, 0.5, 0.5, 0.5])

coefs_matrix = np.column_stack((coefs,coefs[::-1]))

print (coefs_matrix)

Out:

```
[[     1.      0.5]
```

```
[      0.5    0.5]

[      0.5    0.5]

[      0.5    0.5]

[      0.5    1.]]
```

Now we can perform the multiplication. Here's an example of multiplying the array with the vector:

In: np.dot(M,coefs)

Out: array([5.,   20.,   35.,   50.,   65.])

Here's an example of multiplication between the array and the coefficient vectors:

In: np.dot(M,coefs_matrix)

Out: array([[5.,   7.],

```
[      20.,    22.],

[      35.,    37.],

[      50.,    52.],

[      65.,    67.]])
```

In both of these multiplication operations, we used the "np.dot" function in order to achieve them. Next up, let's discuss slicing and indexing.

Slicing and Indexing

Indexing is great for viewing the ndarray by sending an instruction to visualize the slice of columns and rows or the index.

Let's start by creating a 10x10 array. It will initially be two-dimensional.

In: import numpy as np

M = np.arange(100, dtype=int).reshape(10,10)

Next let's extract the rows from 2 to 8, but only the ones that are evenly numbered.

In: M[2:9:2,:]

Out: array([[20, 21, 22, 23, 24, 25, 26, 27, 28, 29],

[40, 41, 42, 43, 44, 45, 46, 47, 48, 49],

[60, 61, 62, 63, 64, 65, 66, 67, 68, 69],

[80, 81, 82, 83, 84, 85, 86, 87, 88, 89]])

Now let's extract the column, but only the ones from index 5.

In: M[2:9:2,5:]

Out: array([[25, 26, 27, 28, 29],

[45, 46, 47, 48, 49],

[65, 66, 67, 68, 69],

[85, 86, 87, 88, 89]])

We successfully sliced the rows and the columns. But what happens if we try a negative index? Doing so would reverse the array. Here's how our previous array would look when using a negative index.

In: M[2:9:2,5::-1]

Out: array([[25, 24, 23, 22, 21, 20],

[45, 44, 43, 42, 41, 40],

[65, 64, 63, 62, 61, 60],

[85, 84, 83, 82, 81, 80]])

There are other ways of slicing and indexing the arrays, but for the purposes of this book it's enough to know how to perform the previously mentioned steps. However, keep in mind that this process is only a way of viewing the data. If you want to use these views further by creating new data, you cannot make any modifications in the original arrays. If you do, it can lead to some negative side effects. In that case, you want to use the "copy" method. This will create a copy of the array which you can modify however you wish. Here's the code line for the copy method:

In: N = M[2:9:2,5:].copy()

Array Stacking

Sometimes, when you work with two dimensional arrays, you may want to add new rows or columns to represent new data and variables. This operation is known as array stacking, and it doesn't take long for NumPy to render the new information. Start by creating a new array:

In: import numpy as np

dataset = np.arange(50).reshape(10,5)

Next, add a new row, and several lines that will be concatenated:

In: single_line = np.arange(1*5).reshape(1,5)

several_lines = np.arange(3*5).reshape(3,5)

Now let's use the vstack method, which stands for vertical stack, to add a new single line.

In: np.vstack((dataset,single_line))

This command line will also work if we want to add several lines.

In: np.vstack((dataset,several_lines))

Next, let's see how to add a variable to the array. This is done with the "hstack" method, which stands for horizontal stack. Here's an example:

In: bias = np.ones(10).reshape(10,1) np.hstack((dataset,bias))

In this line of code, we added a bias of unit values to the array we created earlier.

As an aspiring data scientist, you will only need to know how to add new rows and columns to your arrays. In most projects you won't need to do more than that, so practice working with two dimensional arrays and NumPy, because this tool is engraved in data science.

Chapter 4: The Data Science Pipeline

In the previous chapter, we focused on loading and processing data with Python and various tools such as pandas and NumPy. We successfully created a dataset by creating arrays that contain numerical values, and now we're ready to get closer to the heart of data science. This section may be a bit challenging to the uninitiated, but please take the time to absorb the information, practice it, extend your research towards other resources, and keep trying.

In this chapter, we are going to talk more about data and building new features. We will also cut the dimensionality of data, decrease the number of features, go through performance tests, and much more. Let's dig in!

Data Exploration

When you start analyzing a dataset, you need to perform an exploratory data analysis in order to understand it the best you can. This involves paying attention to its features, shape, confirm your hypothesis, and build your focus towards the next steps. For the sake of consistency, for this phase we are going to reuse the iris dataset we created in an earlier section. So let's start by importing it:

In: import pandas as pd

```
iris_filename = 'datasets-uci-iris.csv'

iris = pd.read_csv(iris_filename, header=None,

names= ['sepal_length', 'sepal_width',

'petal_length', 'petal_width', 'target'])

iris.head()
```

Out:

Now let's start exploring! We're going to start by using the "describe" method as following:

In: iris.describe()

You will now see a number of numerical features, like number of observations, average value, deviation, min / max values and more. Let's get a better look at this data by looking at a graph representation of what we have. You can do this with the help of the "boxplot" method.

In: boxes = iris.boxplot(return_type='axes')

This step isn't in any way necessary, but visualization of data can be extremely helpful. Next, we can take a look at the connection between the features by using a similarity matrix. You can do this with the following command:

In: pd.crosstab(iris['petal_length'] > 3.758667, iris['petal_width'] > 1.198667)

In this example we are counting how many times the "petal_length" appears more than the average of the same count for the "petal_width". This is done with the "crosstab" method, and the result should display that there's a strong relation between the two features. If you want to, you can see the result graphically as well by using the following code lines:

In: scatterplot = iris.plot(kind='scatter', x='petal_width',

y='petal_length', s=64, c='blue', edgecolors='white')

Out:

This will show you that the x and y are in a strong relation. You make the same conclusion as when you look at the data, however, as previously said, visualization is much more helpful.

Next, let's check the distribution by using a histogram. Type the following code:

In: distr = iris.petal_width.plot(kind='hist', alpha=0.5, bins=20)

Why did we choose 20 bins, and what are they? In histograms, bins are simply the intervals of a variable. The general idea is to calculate the square root of the number of observations, and that will be your number of bins.

Creating New Features

You won't always encounter situations where there's a close relation between the features, like in the example above. This is why you need to learn how to apply transformations that will lead to an accuracy improvement. As usual, let's go through an example to illustrate this concept. Imagine you're working out how much a certain house is worth on the market. You have all the dimensions of every room, and from this data you want to create a feature that stands for the total volume of the house. The difference between the dimension features such as height and width and volume feature is that the dimensions are observable, but volume isn't. However, you can determine the volume of the house based on the existing features.

In: import numpy as np

from sklearn import datasets

from sklearn.cross_validation import train_test_split

from sklearn.metrics import mean_squared_error

cali = datasets.california_housing.fetch_california_housing()

X = cali['data']

Y = cali['target']

X_train, X_test, Y_train, Y_test = train_test_split(X, Y, train_size=0.8)

In this example, we import a data set with house prices on the Californian real estate market. To solve this, we need to use a regressor and a mean absolute error of around 1.15. Don't worry if you don't fully understand the code for now. We will discuss regressors and mean absolute errors in the next chapter. For now, it's only important for you to understand the basis of the concept.

In: from sklearn.neighbors import KNeighborsRegressor

regressor = KNeighborsRegressor()

regressor.fit(X_train, Y_train)

Y_est = regressor.predict(X_test)

print ("MAE=", mean_squared_error(Y_test, Y_est))

Out: MAE= 1.15752795578

We have a mean absolute error of nearly 1.16 in the example. We want to try and lower that as much as possible. This can be achieved by using Z scores to normalize the features and make a regression comparison. This is referred to as Z normalization, and it involves the mapping of every feature to new features, but with a null mean and a unitary variance. Here's how this looks in code:

In: from sklearn.preprocessing import StandardScaler

scaler = StandardScaler()

X_train_scaled = scaler.fit_transform(X_train)

X_test_scaled = scaler.transform(X_test)

regressor = KNeighborsRegressor()

regressor.fit(X_train_scaled, Y_train)

Y_est = regressor.predict(X_test_scaled)

print ("MAE=", mean_squared_error(Y_test, Y_est))

Out: MAE= 0.432334179429

As you can see, we significantly reduced the error to under 0.5.

There are other ways to do this and to reduce the error down even more. The process would involve more complex transformations, and there's no point advancing in that direction right now because it's not the purpose of this section. All you need to understand is that applying transformation is crucial for the exploratory data analysis.

Dimensionality Reduction

What happens when you have a dataset with too many features that aren't really necessary? Sometimes features don't contain information that is relevant, and they are basically noise. Reducing this noise is vital because it will make your dataset easier to manage and your data will come out more accurate and with less noise. Dimensionality reduction is just right for this purpose. It is used to eliminate features and therefore improve the time it takes to perform the process.

Covariance Matrix

When you have several groups of features, you will need to search for the correlation between them. This is what the covariance matrix is used for. As already mentioned, one of the purposes of dimensionality reduction is to learn which features have a strong relation with each other. By doing so, you will automatically know which features are of little to no use and you can remove them. We will stick to our previous "iris" dataset where we have 4 features for every observation. We'll be able to use a correlation matrix in such an example and see the results through a visual graph. Here's what the code looks like:

In: from sklearn import datasets

import numpy as np

iris = datasets.load_iris()

cov_data = np.corrcoef(iris.data.T)

print (iris.feature_names)

print (cov_data)

Out:

['sepal length (cm)', 'sepal width (cm)', 'petal length (cm)',

'petal width (cm)']

[[1. -0.10936925 0.87175416 0.81795363]

[-0.10936925 1. -0.4205161 -0.35654409]

[0.87175416 -0.4205161 1. 0.9627571]

[0.81795363 -0.35654409 0.9627571 1.]]

Now that we have our covariance matrix, let's use some more code to turn it into a graphical representation.

```
In: import matplotlib.pyplot as plt

img = plt.matshow(cov_data, cmap=plt.cm.rainbow)

plt.colorbar(img, ticks=[-1, 0, 1], fraction=0.045)

for x in range(cov_data.shape[0]):

for y in range(cov_data.shape[1]):

plt.text(x, y, "%0.2f" % cov_data[x,y],

size=12, color='black', ha="center", va="center")

plt.show()
```

Out:

The result of this code is a heat map, and in it we can see that the primary diagonal value is 1. Why? Because we normalized each feature covariance to 1. You will notice that there's a strong correlation between some of the features, namely between feature one and feature three, feature one and feature four, and lastly feature three and feature four. Take notice that we also have feature two that appears to be independent from the rest that are in some kind of relation with each other. This information can be used to compress the duplicated data and shrink the number down to only two features.

PCA

Principal component analysis, or PCA, allows us to define smaller pairs of features by obtaining them from the current features. These new features are linear, which means that the first vector of the output has the majority of the variance. Vector number two contains the majority of the variance that remains from the first one, and is orthogonal to it. This cycle continues as the next vector is orthogonal to the first two and it contains most of the variance that still remains. Basically, all the data is aggregated to the new vectors created though the principal component analysis.

The idea in this concept is that in many cases, the initial vectors hold all the information from the input, while the rest of them are basically noise. What we need to do is make a decision about how many vectors we can use. We can achieve this by looking at the variance. We're not going to dig much deeper into PCA, because for now you should only concern yourself with forming the foundations for your skills. So let's go through an example where we reduce our dataset:

```
In: from sklearn.decomposition import PCA

pca_2c = PCA(n_components=2)

X_pca_2c = pca_2c.fit_transform(iris.data)

X_pca_2c.shape

Out: (150, 2)

In: plt.scatter(X_pca_2c[:,0], X_pca_2c[:,1], c=iris.target,

alpha=0.8, s=60, marker='o', edgecolors='white')

plt.show()

pca_2c.explained_variance_ratio_.sum()

Out:

0.97763177502480336
```

In this example, we notice that the output contains two features now. We simply applied the principal component analysis object by using "n_components" and setting it to a value of 2. As mentioned, do not worry if you struggle with this concept. PCA can be complex, therefore as a beginner data scientist you should try to grasp the basics of this topic, and perform a more thorough study on the subject once you are ready. Now let's see another example of a concept used for dimensionality reduction.

Latent Factor Analysis

LFA is very similar to PCA because the constraint of orthogonality no longer exists. Data scientists use latent factor analysis when they believe that a latent factor is bound to exist. What's a latent factor? It is simply a variable that you cannot observe directly. With this idea in mind, we can assume that the features are variable observations that are in some way or another under the influence of a latent variable that has a type of noise called Arbitrary Waveform Generator. Here's an example of reducing dimensionality with a latent factor analysis:

In: from sklearn.decomposition import FactorAnalysis

fact_2c = FactorAnalysis(n_components=2)

X_factor = fact_2c.fit_transform(iris.data)

plt.scatter(X_factor[:,0], X_factor[:,1], c=iris.target,

alpha=0.8, s=60, marker='o', edgecolors='white')

plt.show()

Out:

In this example, the covariance between variables is analyzed in the output dataset. We use the Scikit-learn tool to be able to use an iterative algorithm.

Detecting and Treating Outliers

Examples lie at the heart of learning from a data process. If we introduce faulty data that is incomplete, we won't be able to accommodate new data to the result. This will lead to erroneous machine learning algorithms that will cause distorted results. When we have a data point deviation when compared to other data points, we call it an outlier. Here are the main causes that lead to the creation of an outlier. Focus on them, because it's important to understand the source of the problem in order to know how to fix it.

1. The first scenario is that of an outlier that appears as a rare occurrence. In this case, the data is a sample of the original data distribution and the process is identical for all the data points, but the outlier is marked as unsuitable because of its rarity. When this scenario is encountered, the outlier is simply removed from the dataset.

2. In the second scenario, we have an outlier that is a usual occurrence. When you encounter too many similar situations, there is a high possibility of having an error that had an effect on how the sample was generated. When the focus on the machine learning algorithm should be generalization, the learning algorithm in this scenario will learn from a superfluous distribution that is not the focus. Again, the outlier needs to be removed when such a situation is found.

3. The third scenario is the case of a data point that is an obvious error. Usually, there's a data entry mistake that lead to the modification of the original value and changed it to something inconsistent. In this case, the

value should be removed and then treated as if it's randomly missing. It is common to replace this value with an average, however, if it's difficult to execute this path, the outlier should simply be removed.

The first step in learning which scenario describes the type of the outlier is to detect all outliers and find their location. There are basically two methods to achieve this. You can analyze every singular variable at the same time, or multiple variables. These methods are referred to as univariate and multivariate. One of the most common univariate method you already encountered in an early example, and that is the visualization with the help of a Boxplot. We are going to go into more detail on boxplots in a later chapter.

When a data scientist uses this method, they need to keep in mind that outliers can be identified as extreme values. For example, if you are looking at a data description, there might be an outlier if the observation is smaller than 25% - the difference between the 75% and 25% values * 1.5. Similarly, this possibility also exists if you encounter an observation greater than 75% + the difference between the 75% and 25% values* 1.5. This can easily be detected when looking at a boxplot. Another example is when you are observing Z-scores. Generally, if you encounter a value greater than 3, you can suspect it to be an outlier.

The univariate method can expose many outliers, but not all of them. It will only expose the outliers that are represented by extreme values. Those that are a combination of values in several variables will escape this method of inspection. This is what data scientists refer to as multivariate outliers. They can only be discovered by using dimensionality reduction methods that we discussed earlier. They work because they allow us to observe plots of isolated data points.

Validation Metrics

In order to determine how close you are to your original objective, you have to use a scoring function. These are used to evaluate the performance of your data system by dealing with binary classification, regression, or a multi-label classification. Let's discuss and examine some of the functions to understand how to use them in machine learning.

Multi-label Classifications

A multi-label classification problem is when we need to accurately predict more than one label. How's the weather? What kind of career path are you going to take? What type of bird is this? This is an example of such a problem. Multi-label classification is often encountered, and therefore there are many ways of classifying them. Let's go through a basic example in order to gain a better understanding of this concept:

In: from sklearn import datasets

iris = datasets.load_iris()

from sklearn.cross_validation import train_test_split

X_train, X_test, Y_train, Y_test = train_test_split(iris.data,

iris.target, test_size=0.50, random_state=4)

from sklearn.tree import DecisionTreeClassifier

classifier = DecisionTreeClassifier(max_depth=2)

```
classifier.fit(X_train, Y_train)
```

```
Y_pred = classifier.predict(X_test)
```

```
iris.target_names
```

Out: array(['setosa', 'versicolor', 'virginica'],

dtype='<U10')

Now that we have the example, let's look at which kinds of measures we can take for this type of classification.

The first thing we can do is to identify the misclassification of every class. This is done with the help of a **confusion matrix**, which is a table we can use for the previously mentioned step. Assuming that the classification is perfect, the cells of the matrix that are not set on a diagonal would contain 0 values. Let's examine this through the example:

In: from sklearn import metrics

from sklearn.metrics import confusion_matrix

cm = confusion_matrix(Y_test, Y_pred)

print (cm)

Out: [[30 0 0]

[0 19 3]

[0 2 21]]

In: import matplotlib.pyplot as plt

img = plt.matshow(cm, cmap=plt.cm.autumn)

```
plt.colorbar(img, fraction=0.045)

for x in range(cm.shape[0]):

for y in range(cm.shape[1]):

plt.text(x, y, "%0.2f" % cm[x,y],

size=12, color='black', ha="center", va="center")

plt.show()
```

Out:

With the help of tabular visualization, we can see that in our example the first class "setosa" (class 0) is not misclassified. However, "versicolor" which is class 1 is misclassified as the "virginica" class twice. Class "virginica" (class 2) is also misclassified as versicolor twice.

Another measure we can take to identify misclassification is through the **accuracy** measure. Accuracy simply portrays how accurate the classification of labels is. Here's an example in code:

In: print ("Accuracy:", metrics.accuracy_score(Y_test, Y_pred))

Accuracy: 0.933333333333

Another popular measure is the **precision** measure. We count the number of results that are relevant, and therefore the number of correct labels. Afterwards, a calculation is made that determines the average of all labels. Here's how it looks in code:

In: print ("Precision:", metrics.precision_score(Y_test,

Y_pred))

Precision: 0.933333333333

A third measure example is the **recall** concept. It determines how many relevant results we have and compares them to the relevant labels. Basically, the number of correct label classification is divided by the number of labels. The results of this calculation are then averaged like so:

In: print ("Recall:", metrics.recall_score(Y_test, Y_pred))

Recall: 0.933333333333

The last measure worth taking note of is the **F1 score**. This concept, however, is mostly used when we have an unbalanced dataset. The purpose of it is to determine whether our classifier is performing properly in relation with our classes. The F1 score is in fact the harmonic mean of recall and precision. To clarify in case you don't know, a harmonic mean is an average of rates. We're not going to dig deeper into the mathematics side of this calculation. It is enough that you gain an idea of the concept of an F1 score. Here's how it's used in code:

In: print ("F1 score:", metrics.f1_score(Y_test, Y_pred))

F1 score: 0.933267359393

There are other methods you can use in multi-label classifications, however these are the ones you will deal with most frequently. The other step you should take after using these measures is creating a classification report. Here's how to create this report and see the results:

In: from sklearn.metrics import classification_report

print (classification_report(Y_test, Y_pred,

target_names=iris.target_names))

Out:

Now let's talk a bit more about the use of these different measures of multi-label classification. It's worth taking note that "precision" and "recall" are the ones that are used in most scenarios, especially when compared to "accuracy". Why? Simply because in the real world, the majority of data sets are not balanced. This lack of balance needs to be accounted for in data science, and this is done with precision, recall, as well as the F1 score. Also keep in mind that if you get perfect classification results, there might be an error somewhere. In the real world, there are rarely perfect solutions to problems with datasets. The "it's too good to be true" mantra truly applies when it comes to multi-label classifications especially.

Binary Classifications

Let's assume we have only two output classes. For example, when you need to guess the gender. You can use the previously mentioned methods for binary classification as well, however you will have to take an additional step. This step is a graphical representation of the performances of a classifier, and is called the "receiver operating characteristics curve". It's also sometimes known as the "area under a curve". This graphical expression is highly informative because it displays how a change in the outcome occurs when a parameter is changed. First, it expresses the performances of the true positive rate and then the false positive rate. The true positive rate (or hit rate) represents the correct positive results, while the false positive rate (or miss rate) represents the rate of incorrect positive results.

If you search for an example of a receiver operating characteristic, you will notice there's an area under the curve which expresses how the classifier performs next to a random classifier. Normally in this kind of graphical representation, the random classifier is represented through a dotted line, while the better classifier is through a solid line.

You can use the following function to build a receiver operating characteristic graph through Python:

sklearn.metrics.roc_auc_score().

Testing

So far we've loaded the data, preprocessed it, created a few new features, looked for any outliers and inaccurate data points, looked at various validation metrics, and now we are finally prepared to apply the machine learning algorithm. Machine learning algorithms observe our examples, group them with their results, and extract the rules that can be generalized to future examples by guessing their correct results. For instance, the supervised machine learning applies several learning algorithms that can predict future data. The question is, how can we apply the learning process so that we accurately predict the outcome from similar data? To explain this part, let's import a dataset so we can directly work through an example.

In: from sklearn.datasets import load_numbers

numbers = load_ numbers()

print (numbers.DESCR)

X = numbers.data

y = numbers.target

With this "numbers" dataset we are creating a scenario where we have a collection of images that contain handwritten numbers from 0 to 9. Our format consists of a matrix with 8x8 images of these numbers that are stored as a vector. Flattening each 8x8 image results in this vector that will have 64 numeric values from 0 to 16. Basically, this expresses the grey scale tonality of every single pixel contained in the images, like so:

In: X[0]

Out: array([0., 0., 5., 13., 9., 1., 0., 0., ...])

Next, we will upload 3 machine learning algorithms that already have their parameters set to learn. These algorithms are also known as machine learning hypotheses. Here's an example of this process:

In: from sklearn import svm

h1 = svm.LinearSVC(C=1.0)

h2 = svm.SVC(kernel='rbf', degree=3, gamma=0.001, C=1.0)

h3 = svm.SVC(kernel='poly', degree=3, C=1.0)

We are importing a linear SVC, followed by a radial basis SVC and a 3rd degree polynomial SVC. SVC stands for support vector classification, and you can read the documentation on Scikit-learn's website:

https://scikit-learn.org/stable/modules/generated/sklearn.svm.SVC.html

Keep in mind that the purpose of this book is to introduce you to the world of data science and to teach you how to start working with Python. As an aspiring data scientist, it becomes part of your task to conduct the needed research. As the book progresses, you will have to slowly adjust to doing more and more research. We're going to discuss concepts, methodologies, and examples that illustrate them, however as a student you must expand on this data on your own.

With that being said, let's start by fitting the linear classifier into our data and verify the outcome:

In: h1.fit(X,y)

print (h1.score(X,y))

Out: 0.984974958264

The first learning algorithm uses an array "x" in order to predict one of ten classes that the y vector indicates. Then the "score" method analyses the performance of the specified "x" array, as an average accuracy based on the true values given by the "y" vector. As you can see in the example, the prediction accuracy is roughly 98%. This result is actually a representation of how well the learning algorithm performs.

In certain cases, we will not have fresh data available. In such a scenario, the data will have to be divided into a training set and a test set. The training set will contain around 70% of the data, while the test set will contain the rest. The split should be random, however unbalanced class distribution needs to be accounted for. Let's execute the following code see this in practice:

In: chosen _state = 1

X_train, X_test, y_train, y_test = validation.train_test (X, y,

test_size=0.30, ran-dom_state=chosen_ state)

print ("(X train shape %s, X test shape %s, \ny train shape %s, y test

shape %s" \

% (X_train.shape, X_test.shape, y_train.shape, y_test.shape))

h1.fit(X_train,y_train)

print (h1.score(X_test,y_test))

This will return the average accuracy on the test data

Out:

(X train shape (1257, 64), X test shape (540, 64),

y train shape (1257,), y test shape (540,)

0.953703703704

Let's discuss the block of code to see what happens. In this example, we split the total data randomly into two sets, as previously discussed. This is done with the "validation.train_test" function based on the "test_size" parameter. As a side note, this parameter can be an integer that is used to express how many examples we have for the test set, or it can be a float that indicates the percentage of data that should be utilized for testing. Afterwards, the data split is ruled by "random_state" which guarantees that the process can be reproduced at any time and on any computer.

This addition will also ensure that we can run and reproduce the operation on any computer, no matter which operating system is running.

In our example we have an accuracy of 0.94. If we change the value of our "chosen_ state" parameter, we will see a change in the accuracy. What does that mean? The performance evaluation is not an absolute measure and we should use it carefully. Different test samples will yield different results. The performance result should look great as long as we're evaluating on a select test set, however if we use a different test set, the same performance will not be replicated. The conclusion to this is that we need to decide between several hypotheses. This is a common procedure in data science. We fit each hypothesis on the training data and use a sample to compare the performance.

This is when we use a validation set. For this procedure, it is recommended that the total data is split 60% for training, 20% for testing and 20% for validation. Here's how we can adapt our previous example to consider this three way data split and test the 3 algorithms we have:

In: chosen_ state = 1

X_train, X_validation_test, y_train, y_validation_test =

validation.train_test (X, y, test_size=.40,

random_state=chosen_ state)

X_validation, X_test, y_validation, y_test =

validation.train_test (X_validation_test,

```
y_validation_test,    test_size=.50,    random_state=chosen_
state)

print ("X train shape, %s, X validation shape %s, X test shape
%s,

\ny train shape %s, y validation shape %s, y test shape %s\n"
% \

(X_train.shape,        X_validation.shape,        X_test.shape,
y_train.shape,

y_validation.shape, y_test.shape))

for hypothesis in [h1, h2, h3]:

hypothesis.fit(X_train,y_train)

print ("%s -> validation mean accuracy = %0.3f" %
(hypothesis,

hypothesis.score(X_validation,y_validation)))

h2.fit(X_train,y_train)

print ("\n%s -> test mean accuracy = %0.3f" % (h2,

h2.score(X_test,y_test)))
```

Out:

X train shape, (1078, 64), X validation shape (359, 64),

X test shape (360, 64),

y train shape (1078,), y validation shape (359,),

y test shape (360,)

LinearSVC(C=1.0, class_weight=None, dual=True, fit_intercept=True,

intercept_scaling=1, loss='squared_hinge', max_iter=1000,

multi_class='ovr', penalty='l2', random_state=None, tol=0.0001,

verbose=0) -> validation mean accuracy = 0.958

SVC(C=1.0, cache_size=200, class_weight=None, coef0=0.0,

decision_function_shape=None, degree=3, gamma=0.001, kernel='rbf',

max_iter=-1, probability=False, random_state=None, shrinking=True,

tol=0.001, verbose=False) -> validation mean accuracy = 0.992

SVC(C=1.0, cache_size=200, class_weight=None, coef0=0.0,

decision_function_shape=None, degree=3, gamma='auto',

kernel='poly', max_iter=-1, probability=False, random_state=None,

shrinking=True, tol=0.001, verbose=False) -> validation mean accuracy =

0.989

SVC(C=1.0, cache_size=200, class_weight=None, coef0=0.0,

decision_function_shape=None, degree=3, gamma=0.001, kernel='rbf', max_iter=-1, probability=False, random_state=None, shrinking=True,

`tol=0.001, verbose=False) -> test mean accuracy = 0.978

You can see in the output how we distributed the total cases in percentiles to training, test, and validation cases. First, we split the data with our "validation.train_test" function into two different segments. Next, we took the test/validation set to divide it again with the same function. Afterwards, we tested every single algorithm on the validation set. You can see in the results that we have an accuracy of roughly 0.99. This tells us that the best algorithm is the SVC which is using the RBF kernel. Next, we made a decision to use this algorithm further on the test set. This gave us an accuracy of nearly 0.98. At this point, we have to question ourselves whether we used the correct algorithm. Under these circumstances, we have two different results on the validation and test sets. What you should do next is run this code at least 40 times in order to avoid any statistical noise or errors that may interfere with the results. Keep in mind that you should change the value of "random_state" every time you run the code. This way, your results will be as accurate as they can be in such a scenario.

If you don't fully understand the code, try to focus more on the theory behind the concept itself. The point of this chapter is to help you grasp common methodologies in the data science pipeline. Once you understand the topic, you can start slowly building on the practical side of the pipeline. Try to dissect the code line by line, slowly, instead of trying to take it in all at once.

Chapter 5: Machine Learning

So far we've discussed the preparation of data and the methodologies behind it. In this chapter, we are going to focus on the learning algorithms where you will become more accustomed to using tools such as Scikit-learn. We are going to explore and discuss the most important algorithms. Understanding topics such as linear regression, Naïve Bayes classifiers, and k-Nearest Neighbors is crucial to becoming a data scientist. Machine learning is at the core of every project, and is a wide, complex topic on its own.

Because of the importance of machine learning, there will be a heavy focus in this chapter to help you familiarize yourself with the many aspects of it.

An Introduction

What is machine learning? It is a particular category of algorithms that allow data scientists to create algorithms that can predict an outcome based on the data it receives. Basically, input data is fed to the software, and then through statistical analysis an output is predicted. These predictions can also be made on new data that is similar to the old data that the machine algorithms already experienced. The purpose is to analyze vast amounts of information, perform comparisons, tests, and come up with a solid conclusion without the need for a data scientist to constantly intervene. This naturally requires the creation of sophisticated machine learning models that are capable of accurately predicting results on their own.

There are three main categories of machine learning algorithms: unsupervised, supervised, and reinforced learning.

Supervised Learning

In the case of supervised learning, the data scientist needs to provide inputs and outputs that he or she desires, followed by any feedback obtained from the predictions resulting from training data. Once this phase is completed, the algorithm can re-apply it to the next set of data. In other words, it is in many ways similar to a student working under the guidance of a professor. Imagine a teacher giving some exercises or examples to the student. They will then take that knowledge and come up with a set of rules and conclusions that they will apply to other examples.

It is also good for you to know the difference between the regression problems and classification problems. In regression problems, the target is a numeric value, while in classification, the target is a class or a tag. A regression task can help determine the average cost of all houses in London, while a classification task will help determine the types of flowers based on the length of their sepals and petals.

Unsupervised Learning

The key difference between supervised and unsupervised learning is that the learning algorithm doesn't require any output data from the human. Existing data is analyzed and conclusions are made through a process called deep learning, which is iterative. This category of algorithms is usually used in situations involving the processing of complex data. The algorithms learn only from working with examples by recognizing and working out data patterns.

An example of unsupervised learning can be seen in online stores. Someone views a certain item, places it inside a wish list, or purchases it. Based on this information, the algorithms will determine what other items are similar to this purchase, and suggest them to the shopper.

Reinforcement Learning

This category of machine learning is in many ways similar to unsupervised learning, especially because it only needs examples to make predictions. However, the algorithm can also submit a positive or negative feedback. This feature makes it perfect in software that involves any kind of active decision making processes that also involve consequences.

In some ways, you can compare reinforcement learning to human learning, which thrives on trial and error. When humans make a mistake, there's a consequence that can involve pain, loss of money or time, etc. The reinforced learning algorithms sift through data in order to detect patterns and make the decisions and adjustments according to them. Some actions will be more likely to be taken in consideration than others.

An example of reinforced learning is the online advertising system. You bought something online, and based on this web browser history you will receive ads based on the product you purchased, or similar ones.

Approaches to Machine Learning

Machine learning approaches or philosophies can be categorized in a few branches. Each branch focuses on solving a certain type of problem. AI is inspired by human intelligence. Every artificial process in machine learning algorithms in one way or another is set to replicate a human's ability to detect patterns, makes decisions based on available data, and solve problems. So before we dive into the more technical aspect of machine learning, let's understand it better.

1. **Inverse deduction**: Humans absorb data, but often it is incomplete, missing variables, or it's simply erroneous. Luckily, our minds are built to fill these gaps with enough information that can help us make an accurate prediction. We devise patterns even when there are none. For example, the only reason we see a face on Mars is because our mind thrives on making sense of the world through establishing logical patterns. Machine learning algorithms seek to replicate this human approach to filling the gaps in a pattern.

2. **Connections**: Scientists have been working on creating a mathematical representation of the human brain for decades. This is what is referred to as the neural network, and the concept of deep learning is actually an artificial neural network. The neural network is built from nodes, and each node has an input and an output. Sometimes they are in layers, making some outputs become the inputs of other nodes. The training is done through data sets and through each iteration, the nodes adjust to get a more accurate result. Keep in mind that the artificial neural net isn't

an artificial clone of the human's neural network. The artificial kind is made from a series of inputs and outputs with the only purpose of modeling patterns and results.

3. **Bayesian**: This approach deals with uncertain variables by using probabilistic inference. The algorithms update every time there's new data to use, and after a certain number of iterations some hypotheses appear more likely than others. The best example of this approach being used in real world machine learning application is probably the email spam filter. The algorithm processes the words used in an email, compares them with the content of the email, and based on the data it gathers, it becomes either more or less likely for the message to be spam.

4. **Using analogies**: One of the most frequent "tools" for learning that humans use is the analogy. It is much easier for the brain to absorb new data by comparing it to data it already possesses. Learning this way is especially useful when there are gaps in the information and not enough detail is provided. When similar information is available, people recognize the patterns when comparing it to the new information and fill the rest of the gaps themselves with logical reasoning. This approach to learning has also been applied to machine learning algorithms, such as the support vector machine. In the real world, we can see an example of this in application when we look at movie streaming services. Viewer A and Viewer B watch a movie and rate it 5/5 stars, then they both watch another movie and give it 2/5 stars. The algorithm will choose one of the movies that one of the viewers rated 5/5 and suggest to the other viewer, with the assumption that they have

similar tastes.

Keep in mind that none of these approaches can be considered as the best approach when it comes to machine learning. This field is constantly being adapted, and data scientists improve existing approaches and adapt new ones.

Preparing the Environment

The tool that is most important for working with machine learning algorithms is probably Scikit-learn. You may have already installed it by now if you followed through with the previous chapters, because we used it in some of the examples. In this section we are going to apply Scikit-learn's algorithms to some examples, so if you haven't installed and imported yet, now is the time.

As a reminder, you should use pip or any other package manager tool and install Scikit-learn with the following command:

pip install scikit-learn

Once the installation is complete, you can import it to Jupyter by typing:

import sklearn

In this chapter about machine learning, we are going to use already existing data sets that are part of the Scikit-learn library. For instance, we will use the "Boston housing" dataset that used to be available inside the UC Irvine Machine Learning dataset repository. We will use some other existing datasets that are now part of the Scikit-learn library. These datasets are open-source, community driven, and free to use by anyone for any purpose.

Regression

There are two main regression methods that can be used in predicting a value. Both linear and logistic regressions are used in predictive analyses with the purpose to accurately anticipate the results of a particular outcome.

We're going to start first by looking at an example of linear regression. For this purpose, we are going to import Scikit-learn's Boston dataset. It contains 506 samples, 13 features, and a numerical target. We are going to also use the train/test split validation testing that we used in the previous chapter. Keep in mind that in our example, we are going to distribute 80% of the total data to training and 20% to testing.

Linear Regression

Let's import our Boston dataset and see what linear regression is all about! Start by typing the following code:

In: from sklearn.datasets import load_boston

boston = load_boston()

from sklearn.cross_validation import train_test_split

X_train, X_test, Y_train, Y_test =
train_test_split(boston.data,

boston.target, test_size=0.2, random_state=0)

So far we imported the Boston dataset and also created the train/test pairs. Next up, we are going to fit a regressor in the training data set. The purpose of this is to accurately predict the target variable that is part of the test data set. Afterwards, we will measure our accuracy with the machine absolute error, which we also used in an earlier chapter. Errors will have consequences and will be penalised based on their severity. Let's take a look at the following code:

In: from sklearn.linear_model import LinearRegression

regr = LinearRegression()

regr.fit(X_train, Y_train)

Y_pred = regr.predict(X_test)

from sklearn.metrics import mean_absolute_error

print ("MAE", mean_absolute_error(Y_test, Y_pred))

Out: MAE 3.84281058945

As you can see, everything worked as intended and we achieved our goal. You can use the following command to see how long it took to train the system.

In: %timeit regr.fit(X_train, y_train)

Out: 1000 loops, best of 3: 381 µs per loop

As you can see, that was quite fast. Linear regression is simple and offers a high speed of training, however in many cases the results aren't the best they can be. This is the compromise that a data scientists needs to make when looking at linear or logistic regression. So why is it so fast, but inaccurate? The answer lies in the simplicity of the method.

Logistic Regression

The first thing worth mentioning is that the logistic regression is not technically a regressor, but a classifier. It is mostly used in problems that involve classification, namely binary classification, which if you recall only involves two classes. In this situation we normally have Boolean target labels, which have true or false values. These labels determine whether there is an expected outcome or not. To demonstrate logistic regression, we are going to use the same Boston dataset as before.

Our goal in this example is to determine where a house has a value that is either above or under the average in which we are interested. Let's start by importing and loading our dataset:

In: import numpy as np

avg_price_house = np.average(boston.target)

high_priced_idx = (Y_train >= avg_price_house)

Y_train[high_priced_idx] = 1

Y_train[np.logical_not(high_priced_idx)] = 0

Y_train = Y_train.astype(np.int8)

```
high_priced_idx = (Y_test >= avg_price_house)

Y_test[high_priced_idx] = 1

Y_test[np.logical_not(high_priced_idx)] = 0

Y_test = Y_test.astype(np.int8)
```

Next we are going to train the logistic regression and measure the performance by printing a classification report. You might recall this process from an earlier chapter. Here's how it looks:

```
In: from sklearn.linear_model import LogisticRegression

clf = LogisticRegression()

clf.fit(X_train, Y_train)

Y_pred = clf.predict(X_test)

from sklearn.metrics import classification_report

print (classification_report(Y_test, Y_pred))
```

Out:

	precision	recall	f1-score	support
0	0.81	0.90	0.85	61
1	0.82	0.68	0.75	41
avg / total	0.83	0.81	0.81	102

You can see in the classification report that the values for precision and recall are slightly above 80%. Now let's check the time it took to train the system by typing the following lines:

In: %timeit clf.fit(X_train, y_train)

100 loops, best of 3: 2.54 ms per loop

The result is good and the speed is great as well. But why use logistic regression at all? The most important factor that helps us decide whether to use it is simply the fact that it just works in most scenarios. That answer might sound plain, but it's enough to know for now. Performance and speed are great and the regression is easy to apply. If there's a case where the logistic method doesn't offer good results, you can try other functions.

Naive Bayes Classifier

This classifier is a fairly commonly encountered one when dealing with binary and multiclass classifications. It succeeds at probability prediction and is normally used in the case of text classifications because of its performance with large amounts of data. There are three types of Naive Bayes, and each algorithm is used depending on the types of features you're dealing with in your dataset.

We have the Gaussian Naive Bayes, which assumes the features are normally distributed. The second type is the Multinomial Naive Bayes, which is used when the features are counters, or in other words you are working with events that are modeled with a multinomial distribution. Lastly, we have the Bernoulli Naive Bayes classifier. It is used when dealing with independent Boolean features that are the result of the Bernoulli process.

We are going to briefly discuss the Gaussian Naive Bayes and see its application in an example. We are not going to dig too deep into any of the Naive Bayes classifiers, because it would involve too many mathematical explications and that is not the goal of this book. We are going to see only an example of the Gaussian classifier, which is also known as the Normal classifier, to see how it looks in code and give you an idea of its application.

We will use the Iris dataset we used previously and assume that we have Gaussian features.

In: from sklearn import datasets

iris = datasets.load_iris()

from sklearn.cross_validation import train_test_split

X_train, X_test, Y_train, Y_test = train_test_split(iris.data,

iris.target, test_size=0.2, random_state=0)

In: from sklearn.naive_bayes import GaussianNB

clf = GaussianNB()

clf.fit(X_train, Y_train)

Y_pred = clf.predict(X_test)

In: from sklearn.metrics import classification_report

print (classification_report(Y_test, Y_pred))

Out:

precision   recall   f1-score   support

0	1.00	1.00	1.00	11
1	0.93	1.00	0.96	13
2	1.00	0.83	0.91	6
avg / total	0.97	0.97	0.97	30

In: %timeit clf.fit(X_train, y_train)

Out: 1000 loops, best of 3: 338 μs per loop

As you can see from the result, the performance and speed are good, but it's worth noting that we are dealing with a tiny dataset in this case. This classifier is easy to work with because we only need an estimation of the mean and standard deviation from the training dataset.

K-Nearest Neighbors

This is a simple algorithm, however it's used to create complex classifiers that are used in various applications such as financial forecasting and data compression. It's a supervised machine learning algorithm that works amazingly well due to the simplicity of the concept behind it. The distance between a new data point and all other training data points is calculated, and the K-nearest data points are chosen as a result. K can be any integer. The data point is then assigned to a class where the majority of the K data points are sorted.

We're going to use a larger dataset this time to apply the algorithm. The dataset is from the mldata.org repository and can be downloaded and imported directly through Scikit-learn with the "fetch_mldata" function. Just like the Boston housing dataset, this is publicly available. Now let's use the MNIST handwritten digits dataset and see what results we can obtain. Keep in mind that in this example we are going to use only a part of it, specifically 1000 samples in order to benefit from a fast processing speed.

In: from sklearn.utils import shuffle

from sklearn.datasets import fetch_mldata

from sklearn.cross_validation import train_test_split

import pickle

mnist = pickle.load(open("mnist.pickle", "rb"))

mnist.data, mnist.target = shuffle(mnist.data, mnist.target)

This is where we cut the size of the dataset in order to reduce processing

to run

mnist.data = mnist.data[:1000]

mnist.target = mnist.target[:1000]

X_train, X_test, y_train, y_test = train_test_split(mnist.data,

mnist.target, test_size=0.8, random_state=0)

In: from sklearn.neighbors import KNeighborsClassifier

KNN: K=10, default measure of distance (euclidean)

clf = KNeighborsClassifier(3)

```
clf.fit(X_train, y_train)

y_pred = clf.predict(X_test)
```

In: from sklearn.metrics import classification_report

print (classification_report(y_test, y_pred))

Out:

	precision	recall	f1-score	support
0.0	0.68	0.90	0.78	79
1.0	0.66	1.00	0.79	95
2.0	0.83	0.50	0.62	76
3.0	0.59	0.64	0.61	85
4.0	0.65	0.56	0.60	75
5.0	0.76	0.55	0.64	80
6.0	0.89	0.69	0.77	70
7.0	0.76	0.83	0.79	76
8.0	0.91	0.56	0.69	77
9.0	0.61	0.75	0.67	87
avg / total	0.73	0.70	0.70	800

The performance isn't the best, but keep in mind that we are working with 10 different classes in this example. Now let's see the amount of time it takes for the classifier to perform the training, as well as the predicting:

In: %timeit clf.fit(X_train, y_train)

Out: 1000 loops, best of 3: 1.66 ms per loop

In: %timeit clf.predict(X_test)

Out: 10 loops, best of 3: 177 ms per loop

Now we can see that the training speed is phenomenal, and there's a good reason for that. In the training stage we are only copying the data to a different data structure that the algorithm will use later. That's pretty much it. This is probably why data scientists also refer to K-nearest Neighbors classifiers as lazy classifiers.

Now let's look at the prediction speed. We can conclude that it is related to the number of samples we have in the training phase, as well as the number of features. In the previous algorithms we worked with, the prediction phase was different. It was independent and unrelated to how many training samples we had. But what does this mean for the aspiring data scientist? It means that k-Nearest Neighbour classifiers should mostly be used on smaller data sets. They aren't that great when working with vast amounts of data.

Support Vector Machine

This algorithm is as easy to use as the linear or logistic algorithms. The Support Vector machine learning method, or SVM for short, uses little computational power to achieve results with great accuracy. It is a supervised learning technique that has a few advantages over the other techniques we've discussed so far. Firstly, it can be used on nearly all supervised problems, including regression and classification. Secondly, it handles outliers and noise expertly. A third advantage is that it works great with datasets that have more features instead of examples. Keep in mind that this doesn't mean you should skip on dimensionality reduction.

Classification

Scikit-learn offers four different implementations to be used for classifications, depending on the scenario:

1. sklearn.svm.SVC: This is used for binary and multiclass linear or kernel classifications.

2. sklearn.svm.nuSVC: Has the exact same purpose as the previous implementation.

3. sklearn.svm.OneClassSVM: This is an unsupervised implementation used to detect outliers.

4. sklearn.svm.LinearSVC: As the name suggests, this implementation is used only for multiclass and binary linear classifications.

To illustrate the classification with a support vector machine, we are going to use the SVC implementation with a linear, as well as a nonlinear kernel. It's worth mentioning here that the standard SVC's performance is not that great when there are over 10.000 observations involved. Due to this issue, we should employ a LinearSVC instead. Here's an example of SVM in action when using Scikit's iris dataset:

import numpy as np

```
import matplotlib.pyplot as plt

from sklearn import svm, datasets

# import some data to play with

iris = datasets.load_iris()

X = iris.data[:, :2] # we only take the first two features. We could

 # avoid this ugly slicing by using a two-dim dataset

y = iris.target

# here we have an instance of SVM

# we don't want any data scaling because

# we need to plot the support vectors

C = 1.0

svc = svm.SVC(kernel='linear', C=1,gamma=0).fit(X, y)

# this is our mesh to plot in

x_min, x_max = X[:, 0].min() - 1, X[:, 0].max() + 1

y_min, y_max = X[:, 1].min() - 1, X[:, 1].max() + 1

h = (x_max / x_min)/100

xx, yy = np.meshgrid(np.arange(x_min, x_max, h),

 np.arange(y_min, y_max, h))

plt.subplot(1, 1, 1)
```

```
Z = svc.predict(np.c_[xx.ravel(), yy.ravel()])

Z = Z.reshape(xx.shape)

plt.contourf(xx, yy, Z, cmap=plt.cm.Paired, alpha=0.8)

plt.scatter(X[:, 0], X[:, 1], c=y, cmap=plt.cm.Paired)

plt.xlabel('Sepal length')

plt.ylabel('Sepal width')

plt.xlim(xx.min(), xx.max())

plt.title('SVC with linear kernel')

plt.show()
```

As you can see, we first imported all the data we need and then we specified that we want to use only the first two features. Then we created an instance of SVM to fit out the data, but without any kind of scaling of it because we need to plot the support vectors. Lastly, we created a simple mesh to plot in.

In this example, we used a linear kernel. If you want to see the same example but with a non-linear RBF kernel, then simply change this line like so:

```
svc = svm.SVC(kernel='rbf', C=1,gamma=0).fit(X, y)
```

Note on Fine Tuning

Before we move on to the next section, you should be aware of two other aspects of SVM. The first one is regarding variables of different scale. When the algorithm has such variables, it will become dominated by the features that have a larger variance. This means that numbers that are very high or very low can lead to issues when it comes to optimization. This problem can be avoided if the data is scaled to [0, +1] intervals, which is required in order to preserve zero entries. If you don't do this, you will experience higher memory consumption due to how dense the data is.

The second issue is that of unbalanced classes. SVM will most of the time prefer frequent classes. One potential fix involves cutting down the majority class so that it has the same number as the less class. This is called downsampling, but it isn't the only solution to this aspect of SVM. The other option is to weigh the penalty parameter (C) to match the class' frequency. Why? Because the lower the values, the more the class will be penalized, while if values are higher the class will be less penalized.

Once these two aspects are taken care of, you can optimize the parameters. The default values will work just fine of course, but you won't get the absolute best results with them. Let's briefly take a look at the parameters that can be changed in order to reach an optimal performance. We will discuss them in an order based on how important they are for the tuning process:

1. **C**: This is the penalty value, and if you decrease it more noise will be ignored. This means that the model becomes easier to generalize.

2. **Kernel**: This can be set to linear, rbp. poly, sigmoid or even to a custom setting if it's in the hands of a professional data scientist. The most commonly used kernel parameter, however, is RBP, as you already seen it used in some of our previous examples.

3. **Degree**: Other kernels than the ones with the "poly" parameter ignore this because the degree signals the dimensionality of a polynomial expansion.

4. **Gamma**: This is a coefficient for RBF, sigmoid, and poly kernels. You may have already noticed its use in a previous example. The gamma parameter affects how far one training example can exert its influence. Low gamma values mean far, and low values mean close.

5. **nu**: This parameter is used to approximate training data points that are misclassified. It behaves similarly to the penalty value.

6. **Epsilon**: This parameter defines how much error will be accepted without associating a penalty with it.

Since you are only at the beginning and are working on building the foundation blocks as an aspiring data scientist, you should only be aware that fine tuning will become necessary at some point. The purpose of this section is to make you aware of several key aspects of SVM and the parameters that can be modified to optimize your project.

Real Applications of Machine Learning

Machine learning is being applied to every aspect of human life, and you probably haven't even noticed. There are many real world machine learning applications, and all of them are used to make life easier, more secure, etc. Some of them work quietly in the background, while others are actively used.

In this section we are going to discuss the real world

application of machine learning in order to get a better understanding of it. Reading complex theories and analyzing mathematical operations over and over again isn't enough to stimulate your understanding of this concept.

1. **Virtual assistant software**: Are you aware of Siri from Apple, or Microsoft's Cortana? How about Amazon's Alexa or Google Assistant? Chances are you've heard of them, and most likely interacted with them. All of these assistants are perfect examples of machine learning applied in the real world where the masses of individuals use them on a regular basis. How do they work? First of all, you may know you can directly speak to them and issue commands vocally. This is possible because they all use speech recognition machine learning algorithms. Secondly, they are capable of answering most of your questions, because once they process your command, they use another machine learning ability to look for answers. Finally, these virtual assistants will give you the answer, wait for you to respond, perform comparisons with past response, and then use this information to become even more accurate in the future. These tools are perfect "living" examples of all the machine learning algorithms and models we've discussed so far.

2. **Data security**: A great number of web links on the Internet lead to computer malware infections, and this obviously poses a threat to data security whether we're talking about personal users or companies. Luckily, most malware floating around cyberspace is actually old with very minor adjustments. This means that machine learning is perfect for dealing with them. As we already discussed, machine learning algorithms can

learn from past experiences (old malware data) and create accurate predictions that allow them to combat these infections.

3. **Commuting**: Have you used Google maps? It's the finest machine learning example there is. Such applications are capable of detecting your location, direction of movement, velocity, and if you ask for guidance to a new destination, you will receive instructions on how to get there. They can also detect how busy traffic is in various locations, and we're not talking just about road traffic. Have you used Google to check the local gym or shopping mall? Thanks to Google maps, you can also see how busy that place is at certain hours of the day. This is possible due to data aggregation. Data is gathered from all users, and that information can be used to predict how busy the traffic will be in any specific area. But what if there aren't enough users in that given area during a certain day? This is where machine learning becomes even more useful, because it provides the app with the ability to make traffic predictions based on the data from past days at similar hours. Apps like Uber also rely on the same kind of machine learning algorithms in order predict customer demand at certain hours, or decide the cost of the ride based on that same demand. This entire process involves both real time data processing as well as post-processing.

4. **Social media**: We've discussed several times how a significant aspect of machine learning and data science algorithms involve learning from experience. Social media services such as Facebook and Twitter are perfect examples of this simple concept. Just pay

attention to whenever Facebook suggests you people you might know. Their algorithms pay attention to your friends list, their friends, and the profiles you check, what Facebook pages you visit and so on. All of this data is taken in, and machine learning does the rest. This is how the system decides that you may enjoy certain people or pages. Another example is whenever you upload images to your profile. Social media platforms use machine learning facial recognition algorithms to extract as much information from those images as they can. They even focus on detecting background elements to record the geographical location where the picture has been taken.

5. **Finance**: We've discussed so far how one of the main goals of machine learning is to learn enough from experience in order to make accurate predictions of future outcomes. In finance, market prediction has always been a main focus for economists, governments, and even simple business owners. People have always tried to predict the market, but the element with the largest impact over the outcome of the prediction was simply luck. There are too many variables involved in market predictions for people to make an accurate guess on their own. However, that's not the case when we bring machine learning into the equation. While individuals don't have the financial backing to invest in the processing power needed to analyze vast amounts of Big Data, large corporations do, and they use it. Machine learning algorithms are capable of predicting market shifts and outcomes the same way they can make other predictions. One of the biggest problems, however, is a logistical one, because a great deal

machine learning power is needed in order to process the truly vast amounts of market data.

Limitations of Machine Learning

So far we've discussed the advantages and applications of machine learning, however we should also examine its current limitations. Machine learning is not without technical faults.

The first major issue of machine learning is the fact that it requires such massive amounts of data in order to be useful. Machine learning systems are not programmed to simply fulfill a function. Instead, they are trained. That's why we discussed the importance of training data in an earlier section. These systems are trained, and the quality of the training process is directly impacted by the quality of data we have available. With more accurate data, we have smaller margins of error in our predictions. There is, however, another problem within this. Data needs to be labeled first, because machine learning algorithms cannot just process raw data. Training data needs to be pre-processed and label, otherwise the entire machine learning process will be a massive waste of time and money. The issue here is that labeling data can be extremely complex and time consuming. Due to the problems of requiring massive amounts of labeled data, many data scientists consider machine learning to be a greedy system.

The next issue is found in the AI field, where machine learning is a major component. Let's assume that we have trained the nearly perfect machine learning system with massive amounts of accurate training data, and this new system can make astonishingly accurate predictions. What happens if this system is asked to analyze data that is slightly different from what it learned? Often, in such a case, we will get erroneous predictions or even system failures. Why? Machine learning systems aren't humans. They can't fully adapt to new circumstances and use the experience they gained in new, slightly different scenarios. The other problem in this area is that most of the time, you can't train an already trained machine learning system. The earlier experiences will be lost in the process.

Another problem with machine learning systems is bias acquired from people they interact with. This is actually very bad news for areas such as Artificial Intelligence where systems heavily rely on real time data processing when interacting with humans. Once perfect example depicting this problem is an AI chatbot developed by Microsoft. It was supposed to mimic humans and interact with them naturally, as any real person would. The company exposed the bot to social media where it could interact with people. It's safe to say that it didn't take long for the machine learning algorithms to adapt to the real time data they were exposed to. Now you may think that this is good news, because that's what machine learning systems are supposed to do. The problem in this case was that the AI acquired the bias from people around it, and it soon turned into the worst, most hateful social media troll ever seen. This has exposed a significant flaw in both machine learning and AI, especially when a massive tech company of Microsoft's caliber couldn't fix and was forced to disable the AI.

Negative Impacts

Machine learning and artificial intelligence systems can also have a negative side that affects society. As an aspiring data scientist, you should be exposed to these darker aspects as well so that you can limit them as much as possible when you create your own systems.

The best example of a negative impact may ironically be caused by the effectiveness of machine learning. Let's take a look at Facebook. Everyone is familiar with this social platform, but few notice how it works. It relies on machine learning to analyze your interests, the pages you visit, and the people you know, and then uses this data to feed you similar information. In other words, if you're interested in tennis, Facebook will keep bombarding your news feed with tennis topics. This is indeed a well implemented machine learning system that works perfectly - almost too perfectly.

The problem with this example is that the algorithms start building a wall around the user. In very little time, you start receiving only information you are interested in. This sounds good, but this also means you only get to see things you agree with. The system feeds you articles that reinforce your own world view, videos and images that you will like, and so on. This perfect implementation of AI and machine learning essentially creates a massive echo chamber around an individual. Views and ideas that are different than your own will be gone, and this is not a good thing.

Humans grow by learning from each other, debating issues, and criticizing events. Being able to attack and defend ideas is essential to the betterment of society. This learning growth, however, is severely limited when a machine learning algorithm shows you only what you want to see. It almost sounds dystopian, doesn't it? However, this has become a real problem that can only be rectified by improving machine learning systems. In the end, they work as intended, however, they shouldn't entirely rely on your past interests to determine the future ones.

Remember how we discussed that machine learning algorithms are penalized when not achieving a goal accurately, and rewarded when they do? This is part of the problem which reinforces bias. Here's another example that illustrates the issue:

Universities sometimes rely on online advertising to gain more visits to their websites and thus increase the chance of gaining new students. Online ad systems rely on machine learning and algorithms that analyze data that is accessible to them and then form a prediction. They analyze various universities, their departments, and the students themselves, and then point the right ads towards people that fit that training data. The algorithm's goal is to get as many clicks as possible, so it predicts the groups most likely to click on the ads. Sounds like a perfect use of machine learning so far. There's a problem with bias, though. When the machine learning system examines the category of students that is usually found in the engineering department, it determines that it's mostly young male students. This may be a stereotype, sadly, but the machine looks at it statistically and it determines that there's a higher chance of acquiring clicks from young male students when advertising a university's engineering department. The same problem occurs when it focuses the ads only towards women, because statistically nursing schools are mostly made up of female students. Why does this happen? As we already discussed, it's all about the reward. Machine learning has a desire to be rewarded, and therefore it will maximize its chances to receive that reward and avoid any penalties. The same issue occurs the other way around when companies and universities use machine learning to attempt to fight this gender bias. If there's a lack of female students, the algorithm will select only women that fit the criteria and ignore any other segment of the population. The algorithms need to make sacrifices in order to maximize reward.

Neural Networks and Deep Learning

Deep learning is an effective and general purpose way of building new learners in order to solve problems. The concept behind it involves combining all the older learners we already know in order to build a powerful and versatile learner. Constantly creating new, better learners wasn't the most efficient approach to solving extremely complex problems, so deep learning came to be as a stack of all the previous learners. You might've heard about deep learning even if you aren't a data scientist, because it is probably the most popular approach to Artificial Intelligence.

As briefly mentioned earlier, neural networks are a subset of machine learning that uses connect nodes with an input and an output to pass information. One node receives data, analyzes it, classifies it, and then sends it to the next node and so on, going through a long chain of nodes. With every node through which the data passes, it can be further classified and categorized. A neural network is constructed in layers, with the first one being the input layer and the last one the output layer. What we didn't discuss so far is the fact that there are hidden layers in between these two. A classic neural network normally doesn't go beyond 3 layers, however that's not the case when it comes to deep learning. Deep learning systems can easily expand beyond a hundred layers. Let's see how these characteristics represent a neural network architecture:

1. There are at least 3 layers. There's an input, an output, and in between them there can be 0 hidden layers or any number of them. The input and output are usually always present. What's worth noting here is that when the hidden layers are 0, the entire network turns into a logistic regression.

2. The input contains 5 units. In other words, we have an observation matrix that is composed of 5 columns. Keep in mind that the features are numeric and bound to a range of values, usually 0 to +1. This means that any categorical features need to become numerical, and for that to happen the features need to be pre-processed.

3. There are 3 units in the output layer. What does that mean? We have to differentiate 3 output classes, making this a 3 class classification.

4. As for the hidden layer, there are 8 units in its component base. However, this doesn't mean we are limited to having 8 units. There can be as many hidden layers as we want, and each one of them can be composed from how many units we need. There are no rules set in stone for this characteristic. A data scientist is required to decide each parameter according to the each situation that depends on proper optimization.

With that being said, let's discuss a couple of types of artificial neural networks.

Feedforward Neural Networks

This is probably the simplest type of an artificial neural

network. The data goes straight from the input, in one direction, through all the node layers, exiting through the output. This is what's referred to as a feedforward network, and as you can see the name is quite suggestive on its own.

It's worth noting that feedforward networks don't iterate over the data. The input data goes through only one operation instead, and the solution is provided in the output data. This is what differentiates this type of network from the newer ones.

Feedforward neural networks can also be divided into 2 different forms:

1. **Single layer neural network**: If you thought feedforward neural networks are simple enough, they can be even simpler in the form of a single layer network, also known as a perceptron. What does this concept mean? Simply put, there is only one node layer. The input node is connected to a node in the next layer, which has a weighted sum of all its inputs. The node calculates the input data, and if the minimum threshold is met, we will receive an activated or a deactivated value.

2. **Multi-layer neural network**: Here we have at least two layers, usually a lot more. What truly sets it apart is the fact that the upper layer's output becomes the input of the layer under it. This is where the concept of backpropagation is taken advantage of. This means that there's a comparison taking place between the resulted output and the expected output. When an error is found, the data is sent back though the entire network, where the weight of the nodes is adjusted and re-adjusted until the final output result is closer to what is expected. Because of this system, the corrections being made are

actually minute. This means the network goes through a longer process of performing many iterations before we can see it reach a learned status. This type of neural network is considered by many to be the most powerful of the machine learning algorithms.

Recurrent Neural Networks

This type of artificial neural network sends data in two directions, unlike the feedforward networks. However, the most important difference between these two types is that a recurrent network is capable of memorizing its previous states. Data can travel from a later stage back to an earlier stage. Before recurrent networks came to be, the previous neural networks could not remember previous states or tasks. Instead, they had to start all over with a new one. This is like reading a book and as soon as you flip the page, you forget everything you read on the previous page. In other words, a recurrent neural network is a long chain of inputs and outputs. The output of the first input becomes the input of the second, the output of the second becomes in turn the input of the third, and this is what makes them capable of achieving a highly accurate prediction.

Backpropagation

When it comes to neural networks, iterations always produce a margin of error between the real output and the expected about. As we discussed earlier, every layer in a neural network has a weight attached. Its purpose is to adapt the calculations based on what input it receives. This highly mathematical concept relies on probability calculations to determine error between the resulted output and the one we expected. This value is then applied to the next iteration, and this changes the weight of the neuron, which in turn leads to a new calculation with a smaller discrepancy between the results. In other words, the error is reduced with each iteration.

Earlier when discussing machine learning, we mentioned that its purpose is to allow us to create applications that can learn from the experiences that come in the form of data. The same thing applies to neural network, though there is a difference. Machine learning algorithms are tasked with learning how to make decisions based on past experiences. Neural networks, on the other hand, are supposed to "think" for themselves.

Dealing with Big Data

In machine learning, when we refer to big data we're discussing truly vast amounts of information measured from gigabytes to petabytes. Sometimes the amount of zeros that are at the end of a number describing the amount of data just stops making sense to the average person.

The concept isn't new, however. While it was coined at some point during the 90s, the term describes a problem that existed for decades. The concept actually describes quantities of data so huge that traditional forms of data analysis can no longer cope. In other words, when the amount of information pushes the technology of the era to its limits, we can call it big data. There are always points in time when new software had to be coded and new data storing systems had to be built in order to deal with the information appropriately and efficiently.

The Big V's

Nowadays, this concept has evolved to become its very own specialized field within data science and machine learning. The more modern definition refers to big data as any data that contains a high variety of information coming at an ever increasing volume and velocity. This is what sometimes is referred to as the 3 V's in Big Data.

When we talk about **volume**, we mean the actual amount of data that becomes overwhelming to analyze. Keep in mind that this problem used to exist decades ago, before the arrival of the Internet and the growth of Artificial Intelligence. In a world that is governed by tech, the volume of data can increase only exponentially. Many data scientists have debated on this topic and agreed that roughly every 2 years the volume of data doubles, and the speed doesn't seem to decrease either.

Due to consumer electronics, the **velocity** at which new data is being created is astonishing. This has led to the development of new ways to deal with data because it either needs to be processed in real time, or stored for later processing. Storage space, bandwidth capacity, and computer processing power are all being strained.

Another thing you should keep in mind is that not all data is the same. We aren't dealing with just one format. A large **variety** of data, whether emails, stock market data, credit card transaction, etc, needs to be stored somewhere, and each storage system needs to be designed specifically for the form of data it needs to hold. This aspect of Big Data creates further complications on top of the storage space problem.

Data is also considered highly **valuable** under the condition that this value can be extracted. This aspect of Big Data is also heavily influenced by the type of data. If data is not properly structured, it requires a lot of work before it can go into processing. This lowers the value of the data, unlike data that is neatly arranged inside a numeric database.

When looking at recorded Big Data, you should also keep in mind that the quality of it is not equal, usually far from it. The **veracity** of the data from large datasets has a great impact on how much significance is given to certain information. There are countless reasons why data can be considered or suspected to be inaccurate.

For instance, what if those who collected this data have made some assumptions to simply fill in some gaps? What if errors and faulty predictions were introduced in the dataset because of various software bugs? What if the hardware that stored the data suffered from some technical abnormalities? Imagine two temperature measurement sensors that record two different values at the exact same time during the same day. Which one is the correct one? When analyzing the data, you can't determine whether one of those temperature sensors was suffering from a glitch or lack of maintenance.

The source of the data can also be suspicious. What if we're looking at a company's data that comes from their social media? There is no way to verify from the gathered data whether that information comes from real users or bots. And let's not forget the impact that human error can have on data. All it takes is one mistake made by a user of an online service when creating his or her account.

As you can see, dealing with Big Data is no easy task. However, the purpose here is to find the valuable bits of information among the noise surrounding it. Governments constantly study such data to improve performance in various sectors.

Businesses do the same in order to increase their profits, cut manufacturing costs, and make decisions on creating new brands and products.

Big Data Applications

Let's take a look at some of the areas where Big Data can be used to make a big difference:

1. **Predict demand**: Big Data analysis can lead to accurate prediction of a consumer base's demands. We can take in past and present products or service and detect the pattern with the help of machine learning. Finding out the key attributes that made previous products successful can lead us to create new products and services that will have the same potential.

2. **Maintenance**: Big Data is used in pretty much all industries, from tool manufacturers to aeronautics. Analyzing vast amounts of data can help data scientists predict when a certain component is going to fail. Information such as manufacturing year, materials, model and so on can feed algorithms with the right amount of data to make accurate predictions. If such failures are predicted before they happen, maintenance can be called on to solve a problem before it even occurs, therefore significantly reducing the risk of injury or financial loss.

3. **Customer service**: We all know that one way or another, businesses record customer information or acquire it from companies specializing in data gathering. Keep in mind that we aren't talking here about social security numbers or credit card

information. Remember that last time you visited a certain web store, looked at a couple of items, but didn't buy anything? That data is recorded and it is valuable. You might think it doesn't mean anything to you, but companies can get a good picture of their consumer base by analyzing every little action they take. Social media, phone calls, website visits and more are all bits of data that is gathered with the purpose of gaining an edge over other companies. Analyzing this big data can improve the quality of customer service, products, or reduce negative experiences.

Cloud Computing

The Big Data storage problems we discussed in the earlier section is one of the big reasons why cloud computing came to be. Cloud computing involves the availability of data storage to anyone with access to the Internet. It is actually a very simple concept, however it is difficult and extremely costly to implement and maintain. Imagine a large building with tens of thousands of computers working simultaneously to provide cloud computing services. This is the kind of data center it takes to provide cloud computing, and keep in mind that massive companies like Amazon, for instance, require more than just one such data center. The sheer number of machines, electricity, and maintenance represent the muscle behind cloud computing. The reason why such monstrous data centers are even possible is because companies sell access to data cloud storage services to any user, whether individual or a government.

Another massive advantage of cloud storage is the fact that it's an on demand service. Imagine you are running an online business and you are using your own limited server for your website, web-applications and so on. Generally, you don't have a problem with this because you paid for a large enough server, right? Not quite. For instance, during the holiday season, you will suddenly experience a massive surge of customers, so great that it crashes your entire system, thus making you lose money in the process and angering the customers. Cloud computing helps you avoid such a scenario because of this on-demand nature of it. You don't have to spend a massive amount of money to pay for server hardware that you don't need for the rest of the year. Cloud storage systems benefit from something that's called load balancing. The concept behind it is as simple as the idea of cloud computing. When you experience a demand for storage space, the cloud server will simply distribute it to you nearly instantly. When that demand goes down, the balance will readjust without wasting any unused space.

Earlier we discussed machine learning and how complex some of the algorithms are. Data scientists are required to put the algorithms into practice, large datasets with valuable information are needed for accurate predictions, and computer processing power is needed to support everything and everyone involved in the process. As you can see, all of this can be extremely costly, and machine learning is certainly not affordable to small businesses and individuals. It is mostly used by governments, large corporations, and research centers. Cloud computing tips the scales and makes many machine learning features available to any user.

Machine learning systems are used in order to further research in technology, or to give large businesses the edge they need against their competition, however they can also be found as various services part of the cloud. The cloud services can provide any user with machine learning algorithms that are charged per use, thus making them fairly affordable to everyone. Cloud based data storage has become affordable for everyone as well, meaning that all those massive data sets can now be analyzed even by small businesses or individuals because they can be stored on the cloud. The common user no longer needs to worry about storage or data transfer costs when data sets and machine learning algorithms can be housed on the cloud.

This is great news for you as an aspiring data scientist. As your skills develop and you start working with more complex algorithms and data sets, you can take advantage of cloud computing to make your learning process smoother and more affordable. Other cloud based solutions that can help you as a student include software development kits and application programming interfaces. These services allow you to use machine learning functions inside the applications you develop. Because of this advantage, software developers don't always need to learn new programming languages in order to use this new infrastructure. Support is offered for the majority of languages, including Python, making it much easier for any developer or data scientist to use machine learning algorithms inside their own applications. This makes cloud computing a real victory in the fields of data science and machine learning, because most of the real world implementations of these systems involve various applications used for facial recognition, transactions, and so on.

With that being said, let's look at some of the key benefits of cloud-based machine learning.

Benefits

As already mentioned, using machine learning frameworks or solutions can be a costly endeavor even if they are open source and free to use. Working with large data sets and developing AI solutions involves all sorts of costs for hardware, software, maintenance, and even specialists who can maintain everything. However, if you build a cloud based machine learning project, you can use the most limited resources and still be able to run experiments and training algorithms.

Keep in mind that the biggest deciding factor isn't necessarily the cost of production, but the infrastructure. If you work with machine learning the old fashioned way, once everything is prepared, you will need to invest in infrastructure so your software can actually function outside of the system where it was created. With cloud based services, you're just a few clicks away from all that even if you aren't a massive corporation with unlimited funding.

Another major benefit of using cloud services such as Microsoft Azure and Google cloud is the fact that most of the services related to machine learning don't actually require specialized knowledge within that field. You don't even need to know the concepts behind machine learning in order to use them. It's worth noting here that there are two kinds of machine learning services: specific ones, such as Amazon's Rekognition, which is a machine learning tool used for image recognition operations, and generalized solutions that allow you to work with your own code.

Chapter 6: Visualization and Results

So far we've discussed the theoretical and technical aspects of data science and machine learning, but there is one more addition to your skillset that needs to be addressed, and that's visualization. Creating visualizations with Python is vital for any aspiring data scientist because it can easily enrich a project and communicate information a lot more clearly and efficiently.

Visualization involves the use of plots, graphics, tables, interactive charts, and much more. Viewing data through an artistic representation helps users greatly in analyzing it because, let's face it, looking at colorful charts makes things clearer than endless strings of numbers that tire your eyes. Visualization helps with operations that involve data comparisons, complex measurements, or identifying patterns.

In this chapter, we are going to briefly discuss the basics of visualization and explore tools such as matplotlib and bokeh. Knowing how to efficiently communicate information to others is a crucial skill, and even though you are only at the beginning of your journey, you should get an idea of the concepts and tools behind visualization.

Matplotlib

Since visualization is a complex topic that requires its own book, we are going to stick to the basics of using Python to create various graphic charts. We are going to go through some examples with code that will serve as the building blocks of visualization examples.

So what is matplotlib? It is basically a Python package that is designed for plotting graphics. It was created because there was little to no integration between the programming language and other tools designed specifically for graphical representations. If you already became familiar with MATLAB, you might notice that the syntax is very similar. That's because this package was heavily influenced by MATLAB and the module we are going to focus on is fully compatible with it. The "matplotlib.pyplot" module will be the core of this basic introduction to visualization.

Creating, improving, and enriching your graphical representation is easy with plypot commands, because with this module you can make changes to instantiated figures. Now let's go through some examples and discuss the basic guidelines that will allow you to create your own visualization draft.

First, you need to import all the modules and packages by typing the following lines in Python:

In: import numpy as np

import matplotlib.pyplot as plt

import matplotlib as mpl

Now let's start by first drawing a function. This is the most basic visualization, as it requires only a series of x coordinates that are mapped on the y axis. This is known as a **curve representation** because the results are stored in two vectors. Keep in mind that the precision of the visual representation depends on the number of mapping points. The more we have, the higher the precision, so let's take an example with 50 points.

In: import numpy as np

import matplotlib.pyplot as plt

x = np.linspace(0, 5, 50)

y_cos = np.cos(x)

y_sin = np.sin(x)

Next, we are going to map the y axis to the sine and cosine functions with the help of 50 numbers from 0 to 5 that are at an equal distance from each other. This is how the code looks:

In: plt.figure() # we start by initializing a figure

plt.plot(x,y_cos) # next we plot a series of coordinates as a line

plt.plot(x,y_sin)

plt.xlabel('x') # this labels the x axis

plt.ylabel('y') # this labels the y axis

plt.title('title') # we add a title

plt.show() # and close the figure

The result should be a visualization of curve plotting.

We can also use multiple panels to better visualize the two curves on separate panels. Type in the following code:

In: import matplotlib.pyplot as plt

In: plt.subplot(1,2,1) # the parameters define 1 row, 2 columns, and activation

figure 1

plt.plot(x,y_cos,'r--')

plt.title('cos')

plt.subplot(1,2,2)

figure 2

plt.plot(x,y_sin,'b-')

plt.title('sin')

plt.show()

As a result, you should now see a display of the sine and cosine curves on two separate panels.

But what if we want to visualize our data by using a histogram? Histograms are one of the best visualization methods when we want to clearly see how variables are distributed. Let's create an example where we have two distributions with standard deviation. One of them will have an average of 0, and the other 3.

In: import numpy as np

import matplotlib.pyplot as plt

x = np.random.normal(loc=0.0, scale=1.0, size=500)

z = np.random.normal(loc=3.0, scale=1.0, size=500)

plt.hist(np.column_stack((x,z)), bins=20, histtype='bar',

color = ['c','b'], stacked=True)

```
plt.grid()

plt.show()
```

Interactive Visualization

Interactive visualization that is processed inside a browser became very popular due to the success of D3.js, which is a JavaScript library used for creating web-based data visualization with interactive features. This tool is preferred over other methods because there is no latency, meaning data is delivered fast, and visualization can be personalized in many ways.

For Python, we have a similar tool to D3.js called Bokeh (a Japanese term used in photography). This can be found as a component of the pydata stack and is fully interactive, customizable, and efficient. Its purpose is to simplify the creation of visual representation methods that are otherwise complex and time consuming for the data scientist. With Bokeh, you can create interactive plots, dashboards, charts, and other visual representations that can handle even large data sets.

For the purposes of this book, we are going to discuss this topic only briefly and focus on matplotlib-based plots. Feel free to explore this tool on your own, because it is intuitively designed with the user in mind and the documentation for it is plentiful. Let's start by first installing this tool with the following command:

```
pip install bokeh
```

Now let's get ready to put it to the test with the following code:

```
In: import numpy as np

from bokeh.plotting import figure, output_file, show

x = np.linspace(0, 5, 50)

y_cos = np.cos(x)

output_file("cosine.html")

p = figure()

p.line(x, y_cos, line_width=2)

show(p)
```

Let's explain how this code works. We create an html file and upload it to the browser. If you used Jupyter until this point, keep in mind that this kind of interactive visualization won't work with it due to our output preference, which is the output_file. Now you can use any website to incorporate the output. Next, you will notice that there are various tools on the right side of the plot. These tools allow you to personalize the chart by enlarging it, and manipulating it with dragging and scrolling. Bokeh is an interactive tool that can be integrated with other packages as well. If you become familiar with tools such as Seaborn or ggplot, you can transfer the visual representation from them into Bokeh. The method used to achieve this is "to_bokeh" and it simply ports charts from other visualization tools. You can also use pandas functions together with Bokeh, such as data conversions.

Conclusion

Congratulations for making it to the end of *Python Data Science: Hands On Learning for Beginners*! It was a long journey, but it's certainly not the end. Data science is a massive field of study that requires years of learning and practice before you can master it. This shouldn't discourage you, however! Embrace it as a challenge that you can undertake in order to broaden your horizons and improve your knowledge of all that is data science and machine learning. This book offers you the fundamental knowledge you need to get started, but keep in mind that no book or even teacher can do everything for you. You need to work hard by putting each building block in its place as you advance.

Data science is a highly complex topic that has continuously been developed for decades. It is constantly evolving, and it can be challenging to keep up with all the past, present, and future concepts. With that being said, this isn't supposed to discourage you from pursuing this field. You don't necessarily need a computer science degree in order to learn all aspects of data science. What you do need, however, is that spark that urges you to learn more and put everything new to the test by working with real data sets and actual data science projects. Acquire more books and join online communities of data scientists, programmers, statisticians, and machine learning enthusiasts! You can benefit a lot from working with others. Expose yourself to other perspectives and ideas as soon as possible, even when you barely know the basics. The learning process receives a boost when you have other people with similar goals helping you out.

With that being said, let's summarize everything you learned so far in order to put the fundamentals into perspective. Sometimes large amounts of information can seem overwhelming, so let's briefly discuss what knowledge you gained:

In the first part of the book, we ironed out the basics of data science and programming with Python. This book doesn't require you to be a master programmer, but hopefully you practice the basics of programming before diving into the process of data science. In the first section we discussed installing the necessary Python packages and the various scientific distributions that are available to you. Then we slowly moved on to an optional Python learning crash course designed to help beginners understand the syntax of this programming language. You learned about the various data types found not only in Python, but in most languages. Hopefully, you went with every example found in this section and studied them line by line in order to understand how lists, dictionaries, loops, conditionals, etc., are used. Programming is a discipline on its own and learning it requires a lot of practice. You don't have to memorize the theory behind every programming concept (though it can help). The most important thing to keep in mind is that you must practice those concepts. You must learn the syntax, replicate the exercises, and once you are comfortable with only a few of them you have enough skill to create your own little exercises. Python is needed to work with data science concepts, at the very least at a basic level. Many people are intimidated by this topic because they think they need to be expert mathematicians and programmers. It certainly helps if you are, but every skill is earned through hard work and practice. Nobody is simply born with the gift of data science.

In the second section of the book, we began with data munging, the first step in any data science project. We explored the basic process in data science projects and learned about various tools such as pandas and NumPy. This part may require some time to absorb, because there are many tools involved that may confuse you at first. However, in some ways you can compare a data scientist with a plumber in this regard. He is only as good as his knowledge and toolbox. You need to explore a wide variety of programs and tools that are integrated with Python, because otherwise your life as a data scientist will be impossible. There's a solution to every problem, and most of those solutions are found inside your toolkit. You need to familiarize yourself with pandas, NumPy, Scikit-learn, Jupyter, and many other tools in order to reduce the amount of time you work and obtain results with insignificant margins of error.

Next up, we explored the data science pipeline. You learned how to extract meaning from data, detect outliers and deal with them accordingly, and reduce the dimensionality of data. Data exploration and processing are some of the most vital skills you need to gain, and hopefully you followed through with the examples found in that chapter. Even if they are sometimes difficult to understand due to your lack of experience, patience is key. Go slowly, line by line, through all of the code, understand what happens, and do further research to fill in any gaps. Research is something you need to get used to as an aspiring data scientist.

In the chapter about Machine Learning, we explored the many complex concepts behind it. Machine learning is a complicated field of study, and in this section we went through a great deal of theory and technical examples. Do not get frustrated if you do not understand everything at once. Machine learning, no matter how simplified, is probably the most difficult aspect of data science. Due to the purpose of this book, we only scratched the surface to give you a basis from which to start.

We discussed many theories and real world applications in order to help you better understand how machine learning works and how it is applied in real world scenarios.

Lastly, in the final chapter we took a brief moment to discuss the visualization of results. This step is not absolutely necessary to take as a beginner, but you should familiarize yourself with it because it makes the communication of data much easier. Looking at data graphically is much easier on the mind than looking at long strings of numbers and tables packed with information. As a bonus, it's also visually more satisfying to look at a graphical representation of your results after the hard work you put in.

Data science is a complex field that requires a lot of dedication from you due to the amount of information you need to absorb. This book hands you the tools you need to study every concept and guides you with clear examples of code and data sets. The rest is up to you! You have the fundamentals below your belt, and now you can continue your journey to become a data scientist!

23620907R00086

Printed in Great Britain
by Amazon